ECUMENISM

AND

THE EVANGELICAL

J. Marcellus Kik

Author of

VOICES FROM HEAVEN AND HELL

MATTHEW TWENTY FOUR

REVELATION TWENTY

THE PRESBYTERIAN AND REFORMED PUBLISHING COMPANY
PHILADELPHIA   PENNSYLVANIA
1958

TABLE OF CONTENTS

This book is affectionately dedicated to

RODERICK CAMPBELL

who stimulated study on the Coming Great Church

PREFACE

Ecumenism has reached a decisive stage. Either the movement must drive forward to full organic union of all churches, removing and wiping out all obstacles, or it must rest content with some type of federal union. Signs are not lacking that some ecumenists are determined to resolve all differences so that all denominations will become part of one organized church. Others, sensing that obstacles to a comprehensive organization are too formidable, continue to search for some tangible expression of unity. Meanwhile the drive for merger of denominations persists with unrelenting vigor.

The evangelical cannot afford to remain aloof from a movement that threatens to engulf all denominations. He must not only evaluate contemporary ecumenism in the light of Scripture but must declare the scriptural concept of unity and unfold the nature of the church. The evangelical has been sadly remiss in showing forth the teaching of Scripture on the unity of the Church. He must take part of the blame for the confusion that exists.

Ecumenism still lacks an accepted definition. Undoubtedly the significance of the term will be determined within a few decades. The Bible has a concept of ecumenism that does not correspond to the contemporary movement. New Testament teachings on unity and the nature of the Church must be brought to the forefront lest further cleavage results. The duty of the evangelical is to give biblical content to the term *ecumenism*.

Since many have adopted the name of evangelical in this day of resurgent religion, a definition is needed. Historically, evangelical designates one who holds to the absolute supremacy of Scriptures as a rule of faith and practice, and to justification by free grace through faith. An evangelical may be recognized by the fact that he holds firmly to the *sola scriptura* and *sola gratia* of the Reformation.

The author is keenly aware that the biblical concepts of unity and nature of the Church deserve wider and more adequate treatment than he has given. He trusts that more gifted evangelicals will turn to these subjects and enrich the Church with fuller and deeper expositions.

Grateful acknowledgement is made to Mr. Charles Craig for constructive criticism and to Mrs. Carolyn Bateman for preparation of manuscript and proofreading.   J. MARCELLUS KIK
Washington, D.C.
December 1957

Chapter I

THE ECUMENICAL MOVEMENT

The rising tide of ecumenism may in a few generations engulf a number of historic denominations. The movement has grown in power and dimension. On the mission field it has given birth to the Church of South India—a union of Methodist, Anglican, Presbyterian, and Congregational Churches. In Canada the United Church consists of a union of the former Methodist and Congregational Churches and a part of the Presbyterian Church. Mergers of denominations with similar polity, worship, and doctrine are constantly in the process of formation. On June 25, 1957 two denominations of different polity—Congregational Christian Churches and the Evangelical and Reformed Church—formed the United Church of Christ. To some, these mergers and unions are an earnest of a world-wide church. The development of the ecumenical idea has become a passion with many religious leaders and dominates their thoughts and actions. The union of Protestantism has become for them the one hope of saving the world and even Christianity.

Evangelicals—especially those within the historic denominations—must evaluate ecumenism since its promotion and growth will confront them with important decisions. Adopting an ostrich-like attitude by hiding one's head in the sand of indifference may lead to decisions unfaithful to the Lord. Rightfully or wrongfully the ecumenical idea is being impressed upon and fostered within many denominations. Loyalty to the denomination and, more important, loyalty to Christ demand a real appraisal of ecumenism and its implications.

DEFINITIONS

Difficulty in evaluation stems from new connotations surrounding the word *ecumenical*. Thayer's Greek Lexicon states that the Greek *oikoumene* in the Scriptures has the significance of the whole inhabited earth, the world. By metonymy the word indicates the inhabitants of the earth, men. *Webster's New International Dictionary* gives practically the same definition and adds that the word has been chiefly used as a descriptive title of councils that have been convoked from the entire church. Incidentally, Webster's Dictionary defines the word *ecumenism* as, "doctrine or theology of the ecumenical councils"—a sense that some ecumenists would consider with great horror.

Today the word ecumenical is given the implication of unity as well as that of world-wide. W. A. Visser 't Hooft in an article on the ecumenical movement in *Twentieth Century Encyclopedia of Religious Knowledge* quotes from Nathan Soederblom, "The term 'ecumenical' refers to the expression within history of the given unity of the church." Dr. Visser 't Hooft goes on to say, "The ecumenical movement therefore embraces all such bodies as, on an international, national, or local plane, seek to give expression to the solidarity and the fundamental unity of Christians of different confessions and denominations." World Council of Churches' literature seeks to convey that the meaning of the Greek word *oikoumene* refers to the universality of the church. "*Oikoumene* is the old Greek word which refers to the universality of the Church with its many races, nations and tongues and to the universality of its mission as it seeks to penetrate into all corners of the world and into all realms of life" (*Oikoumene, What Does It Mean*, p. 2). "The term *ecumenical* is borrowed from the Greek word *oikoumene*—its meaning is roughly: 'the whole household of faith,' i.e., all races, all nations, and all branches of the Christian Church itself in the world" (*This World Council of Churches*, p. 1). The Greek word, of course, does not have that meaning as used in Scriptures or elsewhere; but that is the connotation the word is beginning to bear in some ecclesiastical circles.

Actually two different schools of thought exist within the ecumenical movement that are endeavoring to give new meaning to the Greek word *oikoumene*. The first would limit the ecumenical movement to fostering good relations among existing Christian churches, manifesting their fundamental agreement, and stressing their spiritual unity. Spheres of cooperation are sought wherein denominations can work for the common good. At the most, if a common structure is desired, the movement would suggest some form of federation wherein each denomination retains its distinct polity, worship, and creed.

A second school of thought would not be satisfied with such a conception of the ecumenical church. Dr. Charles Clayton Morrison disdains this as an amorphous thing that cannot be seen, laid hold of, or grasped. He writes, "It is this amorphous character of the Church of Christ, its formlessness, its intangibleness, its invisibility and its empirical impotence that the ecumenical movement is out to overcome. In a word, the whole aspiration and purpose of this world-wide movement among Christians is to bring the Church of Christ into an empirical existence so that we *can* see it, *can* lay hold of it and so that it *can* lay hold of us and draw us into itself. The goal of the ecumenical movement cannot be envisaged in any terms short of the actual embodiment of the now unembodied Church of Christ" (*The Unfinished Reformation*, p. 54). Visibility to Dr. Morrison is the assimilation of all denominations into one visible, organized church. Others share this view and goal of the ecumenical movement. Dr. John Knox of Union Theological Seminary, New York, maintains in his book, *The Early Church and the Coming Great Church*, that no real union can exist without a comprehensive organization under control of a hierarchy or council.

If the evangelical were to give content to the word *ecumenical* he would define it in this manner: *ecumenism is the movement in the universal visible church upon earth by which, under the influence and guidance of the Holy Spirit, the church comes into the unity of the faith and of the knowledge of the Son of God unto the measure of the stature of the fulness of Christ.* Ecumenists have noted the absence in New Testament teaching of the necessity of one visible organization under central human control. The New Testament emphatically stresses that faith and knowledge form the true basis of union. By mystical union in Christ true unity proceeds. We do not mean to imply that organization is unnecessary. Our Lord has made provision for the functioning of his Church by the establishment of offices for teaching, discipline, and benevolence. However, New Testament revelation does not concern itself with the establishment of a centrally controlled organization, and ecumenists who look upon that as an absolute necessity are turning away from the first century to the second and third centuries for their ideal of an organized church. The evangelical clings to the New Testament for his ideas of unity and organization.

MOTIVATIONS FOR ECUMENISM

Motives for world-wide unity of whatever category are many and varied. They find expression within every group belonging to the visible church. We dismiss the motivation of personal power and prestige not because of its absence but its unworthiness. Both liberal and evangelical circles contain those who love power either from ego or benevolent desire to benefit the masses with their superior gifts. Protestant "popes" prevail among evangelicals as well as liberals. Desire to sway the masses presents itself in the ecclesiastical realm as well as the political. Any movement must guard against those who lust for power and whose motives are impure. However, many worthy motives for greater Christian unity do exist.

First, the world situation presents a powerful incentive to act with Christian unity. Fearful and dreadful consequences of destructive hydrogen and atomic bombs should unite all Christian forces to work together for the elimination of war. Since man appeared upon earth wars have persisted. Ecumenists feel that a united church under one organization would be able to affect the larger affairs of human history and to control events here and now. What the many denominations cannot accomplish in separate existence, a world-wide church with a central organization could accomplish.

Exasperating to the evangelical about those who feel so optimistic that a world-wide church can dominate world affairs and turn them for good, is that they do not spell out how such will be accomplished. Will the means used be spiritual or political persuasion? Being of sufficient large membership a centrally controlled church may be able to exert pressure on the United States government and demand a cessation of atomic tests and the manufacture of weapons of war. But can pressure be used upon Russia or any nation of that type? Will a lobby be maintained in the Kremlin? History constantly reveals that events are often controlled by small groups for evil or good. Hitler and his gang, Stalin and his group, illustrate the influence for widespread evil on the part of a few. Classic illustrations of influences for good are the band of Gideons and the twelve Apostles. Not numbers but the power of God and his Christ are the important factors in controlling world events for good of mankind. God is not dependent upon a world-wide organized church but often uses an individual like a Luther, a Calvin, or a Wesley to accomplish what the organized church has failed to do.

Second, the conquest of the heathen world forms a powerful drive for the Christian church to become united. Pagan and heathen religions present too strong a front for a divided church to conquer. The assertion is made that heathen and pagans would be more impressed and more likely to be converted if the Christian church were one in organization. A united church would be able to wage a more effective and strategic missionary campaign that will hasten the conversion of the world to Christianity.

The claim that an ecumenical church with one efficient organization will effect a stronger missionary campaign cannot be verified by what is happening on the mission field today. Startling and revealing statistics have appeared in the Missionary Research Library's *Occasional Bulletin* (Vol. VII, No. 9, November 16, 1956). "The majority of foreign missionary agencies belong to some association for cooperative effort and fellowship. Missionaries whose boards are related to the D.F.M. (Division of Foreign Missions, National Council of Churches of Christ in U.S.A.) make up 43.5 per cent of the total force. Only a few years ago the proportion was 50 per cent. . . . The proportion of D. F. M. missionaries is now decreasing while missionaries sent by other associations and independent groups have increased since 1952 from 47 to 56.3 per cent of the total. The D. F. M. societies send 631 more missionaries than they did in 1952; the other associations, independent boards, and faith societies send 4,170 more missionaries than they did four years ago." Surely association with an ecumenical movement such as the National Council of Churches does not issue into greater missionary activity. The above statistics destroy the argument that independent or small denominations mean less missionary activity.

An important factor in the greater zeal for missions is the conservative theology of those churches not associated with the National Council of Churches. This should cause soul searching on the part of those who assert that one organization or missionary statesmanship within the ecumenical movement will lead to more fruitful results in converting the world. Not organization, but deep and conservative religious convictions attended by the Spirit of God will bring about fruitful results in heathen lands. Furthermore, a movement that cannot inspire youth to dedicate itself to the cause of missions must always be suspect.

Third, a frequently mentioned incentive to ecumenism is the prevalent secularism. Education, arts, professions, economics, politics, all are being dominated by secularism. Religion is divorced from social, cultural, political, and educational life. More and more secular culture displaces Christian culture. Some relate the breakdown of religious culture to the division of churches which has become a convenient whipping post for all the ills of society. One consolidated church, it is affirmed, would impress a religious stamp upon the culture of the world.

The fact that an increasing secular spirit prevails and the Protestant church is divided into denominations does not automatically relate them as effect to cause. A much better case can be made for the prevalence of secularism in the fact that the church herself has been affected by that spirit. In many communities the church has become a social club and her weekly programs have not been related to the vital message of the church. The church has lost the "saltiness" of vital doctrines and holy living. Merely including all churches under one organization would not revitalize her life and make an impression on the world. This is especially true if the innoxious and vague doctrines that characterize the ecumenical movement prevail.

To overcome secularism within and without the church the vital Gospel message must be preached with power and fearless application of scriptural principles must be applied to the social problems of the community. Not an *organized* Christian society will overcome secularism, but a *regenerate* Christian society.

Fourth, the growing power and influence of the Roman Catholic Church creates a motive for a united Protestant church that has great popular appeal. Alarm has been expressed at the Roman Catholic pressure exerted upon Congress and local communities to obtain favorable legislation to aid parochial schools. Industry and the labor movement have felt the pressure of the Roman Church. Radio, television, moving picture, press, all understand that they must not offend the Roman Catholic Church and hence yield to pressure. Ecumenists have not been slow to point out to laymen that the answer to the influence of the Roman Catholic Church is one organized Protestant church.

The above answer means organizing for political warfare. Protestantism has never taken favorably to the conception of the church as a direct political power and has held to the principle of separation of Church and State. The real and obvious answer to Roman Catholic power and influence has been clearly demonstrated in history at the time of the Reformation. Not by organization but by proclaiming the authority of Scripture and preaching the blessed doctrine of justification by faith in Christ did the Roman Catholic Church receive a blow that was almost fatal. These two notes—most noticeable by their absence in the modern ecumenical movement—accomplished what not even secular governments were able to perform. Also if one desires to match the political power of the Roman Church, one must have a totalitarian church with a submissive people. A totalitarian Protestant church is no better than a totalitarian Roman church.

Fifth, a common complaint expresses concern that divided Protestantism cannot speak with one voice and act with united purpose. An organized united church will provide an effective agency to speak to the world with one voice. Only an ecclesiastically united Protestantism can speak with compelling authority to the press, radio, television, moving picture, industry, and government. This means, of course, a bureaucracy, or a hierarchy, or a council, or a pope to speak on behalf of a united church in regard to social, moral, and political issues.

Whatever agency or agent speaks for the visible Protestant church, the question comes who makes up the content of the message for the one voice to express? Will the content of the message be determined by the membership? by ecclesiastical experts? by theologians? by a hierarchy? Should not rather the voice of God as revealed in Scripture be proclaimed from the pulpits by the ministry whom God has appointed to be his ambassadors? Through the preaching of the Word and the living of the Word influence will be brought to bear on society in its various phases. The idea of a politico-church is a far cry from that church pictured in the written Word.

Sixth, the most powerful motive for the establishment of a world-wide church is the conviction that God desires his worshippers to be within the framework of one ecclesiastical structure. Did not Jesus pray?, "That they all may be one; as thou, Father, art in me, and I in thee, that they may be one in us: that the world may believe that thou hast sent me" (John 17:21). And it states in Ephesians 4:4-6, "There is one body, and one Spirit, even as ye are called in one hope of your calling; one Lord, one faith, one baptism, one God and Father of all, who is above all, and through all, and in you all." Besides scriptural authority does it not seem as though the Spirit is working in the life of the churches to bring about a greater visible unity? A deep longing for visible unity actuates the hearts and minds of many Christians.

No one can doubt that God desires his children to live in such unity and harmony that may be visible to all the world. All Christians should be burdened to render obedience to God's desire and to give visibility to unity. However, the nature of unity needs to be defined and, especially, defined according to the mind of the Lord. The question looms up as to where the mind of the Lord has been revealed—in Scripture or in the religious experience of men? The question of authority cannot be avoided. Assuming that the Scriptures are authoritative in the matter of the nature of unity, then various interpretations must be weighed and evaluated. Does the Scripture call for the establishment of a monolithic church within an episcopal framework or some other polity? Would a federal union of churches fulfill the will of God for visible unity? Or is the nature of unity such that spiritual and doctrinal harmony among the followers of Christ would give full expression to the ideal of unity revealed in Scripture?

EVANGELICAL ECUMENITY

Evangelicals have been remiss in the study of the nature of the Christian Church. An isolated article here and there has defended the viewpoint of spiritual unity among the children of God, but no penetrating study of scriptural concepts has been made in recent years. Showing alarm at the concept of a world-wide church and viewing it as the apostate church of the anti-Christ avoids the real task before the evangelical—revealing the teachings of Scripture on the nature of unity and achieving that unity among the followers of Christ. Castigating movements with no effort to set forth revealed truth and to live that truth accomplishes very little.

As yet the meaning of ecumenism has not solidified although powerful forces exist that would define it as the movement to create a comprehensive ecclesiastical organization under control of a hierarchy. The present theological climate would dispose such a world-wide church to be destructive of evangelical Christianity. Again, ecumenism may mean a determined effort of various denominations to work together for common good without giving up distinctive confessions. A federal union of church may be the end result of this type of ecumenism. Many recognize that federal unity comes short of the ideal. Evangelical ecumenism looks forward to the time when the church comes into the unity of the faith and of the knowledge of the Son of God unto the measure of the stature of the fulness of Christ. This represents the ideal of unity expressed in Scripture. Lower ideals may attract the efforts of men because achievement seems possible and near. Though the road may be long and arduous towards the stature of the fulness of Christ, that only will fulfill the will of God and achieve true unity.

Chapter II

EVANGELICAL APPREHENSIONS

Contrary to accepted opinion, there is nothing inherent in the evangelical position that precludes cooperation and working for the unity of Christ's church. Fears concerning the ecumenical movement stem from deep anxiety for genuine unity and not from native stubbornness. Because the evangelical has deep convictions about Christianity, he desires to ascertain that the movement conforms to the will of God revealed in Scriptures. Long has been the boast of Christianity that of all the religions in the world it alone has received revelation from the living God. This is a firm conviction with the evangelical. He, therefore, compares movements of thought and action with the written revelation. He follows the admonition of Scripture, "To the law and to the testimony: if they speak not according to this word, it is because there is no light in them" (Isa. 8:20).

Lovely and desirable as unity appears the price may be such that no Christian dare pay. Giving up human customs, traditions, ceremonies and adiaphora for closer union would not be objectionable. However, involved in ecumenism are differences in matters of faith, of religion, and of Christology. The whole gamut of religious thought is involved. Thoughtful Christians must carefully weigh the movement and test the spirit to see if it be of God. This may involve a measure of misunderstanding as it is always precarious to question the wisdom and policy of religious leaders and the powers that be. Opposition may call forth the familiar names of reactionary, obscurantist and biblicist but that must not deter from calling attention to dangerous elements in the ecumenical movement.

WHAT THINK YE OF CHRIST?

The greatest misgiving of the evangelical concerns the conception of Christ. To what Christ will ecumenicity cleave? Is it the human Christ of the modernist—an individual without pre-existence, incarnation, and virgin birth? Is it the mythical Christ of Bultmann—a person stripped of all supernaturalism? Is it the synthetic Christ of Professor John Knox—a man whom the community elevated to a symbol? Is it the metamorphosed Christ of Tillich—a human person who became divine? Or is it the Christ revealed in Scriptures—the second person of the Trinity, God-incarnate, Son of the living God, virgin born, Head of the Church, and Lord of the nations? What Christ will receive the pre-eminence in the ecumenical movement? Is there one Lord or many?

In no other aspect does ecumenism betray its naïveness as its evasion of the full answer to the fundamental question, What think ye of the Christ? This question caused several centuries of conflict and controversy but was answered in such a way that it formed a vital part in the unity of the church. In the twentieth century many would avoid grappling with this question as the resulting tension would be destructive of unity. But can the twentieth century church live in an intellectual and spiritual vacuum? How can the question be avoided if the church is to be a confessional church with a definite and clear message concerning Christ to the nations? Some would point out that the question receives a sufficient answer in the World Council of Churches' formula, "our Lord Jesus Christ as God and Saviour." Here the person of Christ is described as God and his function as Saviour. The present theological climate demands a more definite and detailed answer. Every word in the formula has diversities of interpretation—some of which strike at the very foundation of Christianity. Heresies have not evaporated in the course of centuries and the church must protect her precious revealed truths with clear-cut teachings. The occasion for creeds has not disappeared.

The fallaciousness of thinking that divergent views of Christ may harmoniously exist in one church must certainly be apparent. Much has been written that the ecumenical church would be enriched by different beliefs. An accepted dogma of the ecumenical movement teaches that the Holy Spirit is the author of diversity as well as uniformity. However, let not diversities of belief concerning the person and work of Christ be thrust upon the Spirit. He authors unity of faith and not confusion of beliefs. He does not reveal to the church a human Christ, a mythical Christ, a synthetic Christ, a metamorphosed Christ, and the divine Christ. Why must human error and confusion be thrust upon the Holy Spirit? Encouraging persons of opposite tenets to believe that each might find shelter under the ecumenical umbrella under the pretext of establishing unity, will prove eventually to be destructive of concord and harmony. Imagine an evangelical preacher indoctrinating his congregation with the Nicene and Chalcedon definitions of the Christ and then be succeeded by one who would declare this teaching false, alleging that Christ is not of the same essence as God. What confusion and disunity would this establish in the congregation!

The evangelical has no assurance that his view of Christ will prevail if he entered into the projected world-wide church. A battle will ensue for the control of theological seminaries. An intimation of what will happen is given by Clayton C. Morrison, "And there can be no united church without a ministry that is ecumenically minded and ecumenically accepted. The maintenance of denominational theological schools for the training of a denominationally minded ministry obviously has the effect of perpetuating division in the Church of Christ. The ecumenical ideal requires the abandonment of this organ of denominationalism and the transformation of its theological seminaries into ecumenical institutions" (*The Unfinished Reformation*, pp. 59, 60). Apparently no "divisive" theology will be taught. Certainly professors would not be compelled to teach all views of Christ, especially *as truth*. Even a chameleon would become neurotic on such a patchwork of colors. The very essence of Christianity is bound up with the estimate of the person of Christ and the evangelical must have definite assurance that the scriptural view will prevail.

THEOLOGY MINIMIZED

Theology has been termed the great divider. Ecumenists evidence chariness of theology since it has separated great bodies of people into different denominations. To achieve unity they feel a necessity to belittle theology's importance. Many have given up all thought of achieving unity on basis of theological agreement. This disconcerts the evangelical for actually theology has been the great unifier rather than divider. Distinctive doctrines have welded together millions of people. Large denominations have not been formed by hazy and indefinite theology and that factor is often forgotten or ignored. Theology in its simple meaning signifies religious knowledge of God and may also be defined as that deductive science that methodically formulates religious truth. To the evangelical the premises of that deductive science are supplied mainly by authoritative revelation in Scripture; for others the premises are found in religious experience. True knowledge of God, simply or scientifically stated, unifies. Hazy, indefinite theology has no cohesive power. False theology disrupts and causes disunity.

Although this age witnesses a return to theology, and biblical theology, yet much ecumenical literature depreciates this science lest the formation of a common church structure be hindered. Pure religion rather than theology receives emphasis as being of prime importance. Yet theology is indispensable in communicating religion to the minds and hearts of men. To obtain religion without theology is like asking to make bricks without clay. The theology of the ecumenical movement will stamp the character of the future church and determine whether its religion be pure or adulterated, true or false, scriptural or unscriptural. Theology must be emphasized for it is vital to true religion.

The evangelical finds the chief source of his theology in holy Scriptures. While unity, harmony, and peace are devoutly to be desired, truth is still more so. The order revealed by the Spirit must not be forgotten, "The wisdom which is from above is first *pure*, then peaceable" (James 3:17). Peace should be zealously sought but always in subordination to revealed truth. Every attempt to reconcile the differences among Christians that involves the sacrifice of truth or the least deliberate deviation from the revealed will of God, is dangerous and must be resisted. Actually it carries the seeds of discord.

Denominations have been the target for much criticism that their theological differences have been the great cause of disunion. Nothing is further from the truth. Through their theological emphasis the Lutheran, Methodist, Episcopal, Baptist, Presbyterian and other denominations have united large numbers of people. The theological emphasis has been a rallying point and not divisive. Where theology has been neglected, ignored, or minimized community and independent churches have mushroomed. Contrary to popular opinion, theology has manifested itself as a unifying influence. Minimizing theology will produce a weak and spineless religion that has little resemblance to the strong and valiant Christianity that conquered pagan Rome and heathen nations.

ECUMENICAL INCLUSIVENESS

The inclusiveness of the ecumenical movement causes great misgiving to the evangelical. What seems virtuous, praiseworthy, and unifying to the ecumenist appears evil, blameworthy, and divisive to the evangelical. A most frequently mentioned concern has been the composition of leadership in the movement for a world-wide church. Outstanding liberals have held prominent official positions in Church Councils that are recognized as nurturing the ecumenical movement. Some of the radical liberals have issued statements that seem destructive of biblical Christianity. True, evangelicals have often been careless in considering statements of individual leaders as official pronouncements of church councils. Nevertheless, the composition of a group does indicate its direction and character. Official constitutions and creeds have not always restrained organizations from going in an opposite direction and changing their character.

No one will argue that the general tenor of the ecumenical movement is to include a wide variety of beliefs. C. C. Morrison writes, "What, in a united church, shall we do with our differences? There can be only one answer. They must be welcomed and embraced as essential to the fulfillment of the Christian life. Our diversities are not a spiritual liability, but a spiritual asset, of the Christian life. They do not derogate from our unity; they contribute to it. Embraced in the ecumenical church, these diversities, freely intermingling and interacting, would stimulate, guide and enhance its spiritual life beyond anything we have known in our sectarian separation." (*The Unfinished Reformation*, p. 82). Seemingly, diversities of belief are a spiritual asset; diversities of governments are a spiritual liability. We need not have one unifying faith; we must have one unifying organization. External unity possesses more importance than inward unity of faith.

While minor differences of beliefs may be included in a Christian movement, surely not major. The evangelical movement has been guilty of separation on apparently minor differences. Of course, real argument issues as to what may be considered a minor or major difference of belief. According to the creeds of historic denominations the norm for judgment is Scripture. The question of authority itself must be considered of prime importance and vital to the very existence of Christianity. The Trinity, origin, essence, and destiny of man, sin and death, salvation, nature of the Church, sacraments, justification, sanctification, judgment, resurrection, eternal life—all have been considered by the church to be of paramount importance. The suggestion to find union by "agreeing to disagree" on vital doctrines is unworthy of the Christian church. These concern her confession, her testimony, her witness to the world. An uncertain sound emanating from the church concerning matters that are at the heart and life of her existence will fail to arouse the world to the need of embracing Christianity.

How can the church tolerate differences of belief concerning that which the New Testament has declared vital for salvation? One clear teaching of the written Word indicates that mankind is redeemed with the precious blood of Christ, as of a lamb without blemish and without spot (I Pet. 1:18, 19). Some within the visible church find that teaching abhorrent and will not proclaim it. Yet the New Testament abounds with passages on the blood of Christ: *blood of the new covenant for remission of sin* (Matt. 26:28); *this cup is the new covenant in my blood* (Luke 22:20); *the church purchased with his own blood* (Acts 20:28); *propitiation through faith in his blood* (Rom. 3:25);

justified by his blood (Rom. 5:9); *communion of the blood of Christ* (I Cor. 10:16); *redemption through his blood* (Eph. 1:7); *made nigh by the blood of Christ* (Eph. 2:13); *washed us from our sins in his own blood* (Rev. 1:5); *redeemed us to God by the blood* (Rev. 5:9); *overcame him by the blood of the Lamb* (Rev. 12:11). On the basis of these scriptural teachings and others, the evangelical preaches the vicarious substitutionary atonement of our Lord. This view of the atonement is organically integrated in the system of federal theology. Those who hold to to the system of federal theology cannot conceive of any other view. To them one of the foundation stones of Christianity crumbles with rejection of the substitutionary atonement of Christ. A church that refuses to declare what is vital for salvation under the pretext of achieving unity is both cowardly and unfaithful to her God-given mission of being a pillar for truth.

What relates to the doctrine of salvation relates to other vital doctrines. Opposite opinions will weaken and destroy the foundations of our Christian faith. The very substance of Christianity will be lost if truth be sacrificed to obtain peace and union. At the most it would be an outward, hollow show of harmony. To encourage persons of opposite tenets to believe that each might find shelter under the wings of an ecumenical church and live in peace and harmony is a vain delusion.

CONCEPTION OF CHURCH

Two points of emphasis in regard to the nature of the Church give great concern as ecumenical literature is carefully studied. The first concerns the acceptance of the Roman Catholic view of the church as a visible society. The second relates to the growing view of the church as an institution.

The Roman Catholic Church has maintained, in opposition to the Protestant position, that visibility, as including one external organization, is an essential property of the Church. This external society possesses all the attributes, prerogatives, and promises of the true church and all outside of its pale perish. Protestantism has maintained that the church is the company of believers, called out of the evil world, and bound to Christ through living faith. Regardless of ecclesiastical organization those united with Christ are eternally saved and form the Body of Christ upon earth. The attributes, prerogatives, and promises belong to the true children of God and not to any particular external society as such. The external church contains those who are hypocrites and immoral and therefore cannot be equated with the true Church of God. Protestant theologians have formulated the conception of the invisible Church to conform to teaching of Scripture. (See Chapter X, Invisible And Visible). The modern ecumenical emphasis on the absolute necessity of one external organization has close affinity with the Roman Catholic position.

The almost hysterical plea for organizational unity would make it appear that the church depends upon a human institution for life and influence. God stands helpless, it seems, until the church is properly functionalized with efficient secretaries to direct all activities. The salvation of souls, the promotion of true religion, the implanting of holiness—all must wait proper and full achievement until one ecclesiastical machine be provided. The reigning Christ, head over all things to the church, the indwelling Holy Spirit, the Gospel of power seem relatively unimportant to the master architects and builders of the monolithic church. The voice of Christ declaring, "I will build *my* church," is scarcely heard above the babel shouting: "*We* will build *the* church." "Not by might, nor by power, but by my spirit" has little acceptance with those who stress "might and power through organization." "The Gospel of Christ, the power of God unto salvation" has little appeal to men engrossed with "the gospel of unification, the power for the salvation of the world." However, neither God the Father, nor God the Son, nor God the Holy Spirit, are subject to institutional control.

OTHER APPREHENSIONS

Fear has been expressed that churches seek unity from a realization of dwindling strength and influence. Instead of acknowledging that weakness has resulted from a bankrupt Liberalism and catering to the wisdom of men, the church seeks to bolster its waning influence by show of numbers.

The movement is suspect because the clergy are prime movers. The grass roots of the church are unaffected and move in the direction of amalgamation purely through ignorance and indifference. A centrally controlled church will undoubtedly mean extension of clerical control.

Bureaucracy seems to be the inevitable result of large organizations. A general synod or assembly would only exist to ratify decisions reached by a few—well intentioned though such decisions might be.

Not to be forgotten is the divisiveness of ecumenical movements. In Canada the movement for a united church divided friends, families, communities, and churches. Though occuring in 1925, time has not healed all wounds. The ecumenical movement in the United States has disrupted the life and work of many denominations and caused great bitterness.

The evangelical fears that the ecumenical movement may separate the twentieth century church from the gains of the past. Providence has led the church through controversies that have separated heresy from truth, chaff from wheat, dross from gold. The church through the centuries has grown in the faith and knowledge of the Lord Jesus Christ. From maturity the church seems to have returned to the state of childhood as again questions of Christology, nature of the Church, content of faith—defined clearly in historic creeds—are discussed and debated anew without recourse to past achievements. If new light from Scripture were brought to the fore there would be no concern as all creeds are fallible and must constantly be judged and reviewed in the light of the written revelation. But ancient and hoary heresies, dressed in new paradoxical and existential garments, are paraded and received with great awe and reverence. Ecumenism goes deeper than just the desire for organizational unity; the movement seeks to embrace that which the evangelical fears will destroy the foundation of Christianity.

As apprehensions are expressed, charges will be leveled that the evangelical possesses the seven demons of stubbornness, disunity, reaction, intolerance, independency, obscurantism, and biblicism. However, acknowledging weaknesses and imperfections, the evangelical does concern himself with unity as the evangelical movement has done throughout the centuries. He feels that the standard of unity expressed in Scripture is of a higher nature and more lasting than much of that expressed in ecumenical literature. He hopes to do more than just condemn, rather to point to that unity of which the Holy Spirit is the author.

Chapter III

IS DENOMINATIONALISM SINFUL?

Unhappy divisions—fragmented body—intolerable divided Protestantism—broken fellowship—ecclesiastical zoo—endless fissiparation—split and splintered—divided and torn—greatest scandal of civilization—perverse spirit of sectarianism—wilderness of sectarianism—proliferation of sectarianism—unregenerated nineteenth century sectarianism—sectarian fragmentation of the Christian fellowship—apostate denominational system—destructive denominational rivalries—scandal of a divided Christendom—scattered fragments of the Body of Christ—dismemberment and disunity of His body—Christian disunity an intolerable anomaly—divisions are unnecessary, unworthy, deplorable, and actual sinful—divisions within its own life as a violent contradiction of its own fundamental nature.

These common and recurring vivid phrases and sentences describing denominationalism rival the portrait of the apocalyptic Scarlet Woman of the book of Revelation, "And I saw a woman sit upon a scarlet coloured beast, full of names of blasphemy. . . . having a golden cup in her hand full of abominations and filthiness of her fornication. . . . the Mother of harlots and abominations of the earth." Denominationalism, according to some ecumenists, is full with names of blasphemy and holds a cup of abominations.

If the descriptive expressions occurring so frequently in ecumenical literature were to be taken seriously, then all Protestant denominations should flee back to the Roman Catholic Church, for she does not show the terrible "sin" of organizational disunity. She may have mothered many abominations, but not the "greatest scandal of Christendom"—organizational disunity!

Something, however, seems definitely wrong with this evaluation of denominationalism. Living in scandalous sin and fragmenting the body of Christ, as asserted, are terrible charges and should not be assumed true until definitely proved. If true, they are sufficiently heinous sins to exclude the guilty from the kingdom of heaven. Frequent repetition has caused the assumption that the charges are factual. But those who accuse denominationalism of sin seldom explain *how* it constitutes sin and *how* it fragments the body of Christ. Some denominations were formed with deep conviction of the guidance of the Holy Spirit and with a price of suffering and blood. The certainty of the founders of denominations that they were in the will of God must be weighted against the conviction that such were fragmenting the Body of Christ.

CATEGORICAL YES AND NO

The answer to the question of sinfulness of denominationalism does not lie within the categorical yes and no. The color cannot be determined black or white but takes on the hue of grey, either dark or light, as the case may be. The earthly state of the church prevents almost any action from being sinless. Yet the presumption must not be made, as it often is, that the color is dark grey. Denominationalism does not deserve to be called indicative of an apostate spirit.

Who would assume that Luther and Calvin acted under an evil impulse in breaking away from the Church of Rome? To have remained in a church that deserted the teachings of Scripture would have been a terrible sin, especially since that church resisted reformation. Anglicans feel that it was more than the political and domestic interests of King Henry VIII that severed the English church from Rome. Baptists and Congregationalists were led by strong convictions of scriptural teachings to establish new denominations. And who can doubt that providential leadings, rather than an evil spirit, brought about the establishment of many denominations?

Divisions purely geographical cannot be classified as sinful. The Presbyterian and Reformed denominations furnish one example out of many. Those holding to the Reformed faith exist in various countries: France, Hungary, Holland, Great Britain, United States, Canada, New Zealand, Australia and other lands. Assuming that they are all faithful to their Confessions and are like-minded in doctrine, worship, government and discipline, surely their geographical divisions do not take on the nature of sin. All have their own organizations and are independent of each other; but according to their standards, all proclaim the same gospel, all worship in same manner, all uphold government by presbyters. Thus they maintain a Reformed unity that is visible and recognizable.

But could not all these geographical divisions of the Presbyterian and Reformed bodies be made into one by a central organization? Would that not give more strength and visible unity? While at first glance a large organization may seem to possess greater strength, it must always be remembered that the church is not a political organization that obtains strength from numbers and efficient human control; the church is a spiritual organization that receives strength from God. Central organizations suffer from bureaucracy that often hinders the life of the church. Take the missionary representation of three Presbyterian bodies as an example. According to the Missionary Research Library of New York City, the Presbyterian Church U. S. A. in 1956 sent out 1,072 missionaries, the Presbyterian Church U. S. (Southern) sent out 477, and the United Presbyterian Church sent out 265. Yet the membership of the Presbyterian Church U. S. A. is triple that of the Southern Church and 10 times that of the United Presbyterian Church. Proportionately the larger body sent out 21 per cent less missionaries than the Southern Church and 73 per cent less than the United Presbyterian Church. While it may be argued fairly that the larger number of missionaries by the smaller denominations is due to a greater conservative element, nevertheless it nullifies the argument that more powerful and efficient work can be done by a large organization with central control.

The mind of the Lord that large organizations are not necessary to advance his work has been revealed in Scripture and history. The Lord instructed Gideon to reduce the thousands of Israelites to the number of 300 and wrought a victory against a mighty pagan foe who were as locusts in numbers. The Word of the Lord revealed to Zerubbabel, "Not by might, nor by power, but by my spirit, saith the Lord of hosts" (Zech. 4:6). The Lord left the ecclesiastical structure of the Jewish church and endued a handful of apostles with the Spirit and power. The Lord left the ecclesiastical organization of the Roman Catholic Church and caused Luther and Calvin to bring forth the Reformation. John Wesley, with a few comrades, was chosen to stir up England when the organized church was immobilized by worldliness and spiritual deadness.

The apostle John once said to Jesus, "Master, we saw one casting out devils in thy name; and we forbade him, because he followeth not with us." At that time John was irked that someone not in the same association was actually casting out devils in the name of Christ. Even though this individual was accomplishing good, John forbade him because, as we might say today, he was not in the same church. Jesus rebuked John, "Forbid him not: for he that is not against us is for us." The important point with Christ was not organizational unity but that devils were being cast out in his name. The individual was doing the identical work as the disciples, even though he was not associated with the same group. Even so today, far more importance should be attached to the casting out of devils in the name of Christ, than in the effort to create one smooth and centrally controlled organization. Often the smaller denominations evidence greater activity in casting out devils prevalent in the world, than do the larger denominations. In Christian work quality counts far more than quantity.

For more effective organization and efficiency the Lord divided the small nation of Israel into 12 tribes, each having its own government. But did they not have one king who molded them into an organized kingdom? Yes, but that desire to have a visible king was against the will of God and finally caused division into two kingdoms. The Israelites rebelled against the theocratical government and wanted a visible head. One wonders how much of the nature of the ancient Israelite is in the ecumenical movement with its passion for a visible central organization.

After all, the new Israel has Christ as King and, though at the right hand of God in heaven, he rules over the Church and provides her with strength and glory.

Much can be said for small church organizations. The danger of central directives by a bureaucracy is eliminated. Efficient church board secretaries just love to do the thinking for ministers and often kill individual initiative. In a small denomination both laity and ministry have a feeling of family relationship that becomes lost in a huge organization. More opportunities for developing leadership prevail. Small church bodies have shown themselves to be more effective in recruiting youth for the ministry and the missionary field.

ELEMENT OF SIN

While existence of many church organizations does not necessarily take on the nature of sin, and actually has proven to be a blessing to the visible church on earth, the different conceptions of organization, doctrine, and worship do reflect an element of sin. These differences, at least in the past, have been honest differences, originating from a sense of faithfulness to the written Word of God. Man's imperfection, lack of wisdom, and diverse apprehensions of Scripture, have prevented similarity of organization, unity of faith, and identical worship. Knowing the deficiency of man and his deep-rooted sin, the wonder is not the number of denominations that exist, but that not more have come into being. Little consideration has been given to the large numbers that have found themselves like-minded in regard to polity, doctrine, and worship, and have found their spiritual homes within the Episcopal, Baptist, Presbyterian, Methodist, Pentecostal, Congregational and other churches. As long as different interpretations of Scriptures prevail, denominations will be found to propagate them.

A proffered solution, and one very popular today, suggests that differences be forgotten and unity achieved on the things wherein agreement exists. This seemingly simple solution has a multitude of perplexing hindrances. For instance, within what framework of polity would unity be accomplished? Broadly speaking, three systems of church organization exist—congregational, presbyterian, and episcopal. All three claim scriptural authority and contend that if not belonging to the *esse* of the church, at least they belong to the *bene esse*. The achievement of organizational unity means that two of these systems must yield to a third. Strong voices urge the adoption of the episcopal system of church government. John Knox writes in support of adopting the historic episcopacy, "I simply cannot conceive of the union of Christendom except on the ground of a polity which, while not failing to embody the invaluable contributions of groups with a presbyterian or congregational tradition, yet involves the full acceptance of the historic episcopate" (*The Early Church*, p. 142). On this basis there would be no "invaluable contributions" of groups with presbyterian or congregational tradition as far as polity is concerned. Presbyterian and congregational polity would cease to exist. As in a nation you cannot have an oligarchy—the rule of few—and a democracy at the same time; neither can you have an episcopal, presbyterian, and congregational polity existing at the same time. While some may be willing to "sacrifice" their polity for the sake of unity, others feel that they would be disloyal to the revealed will of God in Scriptures.

More than polity becomes involved in organizational unity if the union takes the form of the historic episcopate. The nature of the ministry and of the church are very much involved. In regard to the ministry, Dr. William Cunningham asks the pertinent question, "Should there exist permanently in the church of Christ a separate and distinct order of ordinary office-bearers superior to pastors, invested with jurisdiction over them, and possessed of the exclusive right of performing certain functions which are essential to the preservation of an organized church, and the ordinary administration of ecclesiastical affairs?" (*Historical Theology*, Vol. I, p. 234). Many deny that the Scriptures call for a separate and distinct order of office-bearers and that an uninterrupted succession of ordination by bishops is essential to the ministry. Many hold that ordination confers neither grace nor office, but is the solemn recognition of the calling of the Holy Spirit. Thus the acceptance of the historic episcopate would call for the rejection of historic positions on the part of major denominations—positions that they have maintained as based on Scripture.

Involved, also, is the conception of the nature of the church. Anglicans understand by the Church an external society professing the true faith, united in the communion of the same sacraments, and subjection to bishops canonically ordained. They would urge that to keep the continuity of the church the episcopacy be accepted and all ministers receive ordination from Anglican or Episcopal Bishops. There are those within the Anglican communion who attribute the view of episcopacy as the essential apostolic ministry to the party of Anglo-Catholics. Philip Edgecumbe Hughes writes, "It must be emphasized, however, that this is not the view of historic Anglicanism, in which *faith*, agreement on *doctrine*, has always been given precedence over considerations of order. Thus, though the Church of England is an episcopal Church believing fully that the threefold ministry is agreeable to Holy Scripture, its Thirty-Nine Articles of Religion do not so much as mention Episcopacy as a necessary mark of church and ministry" (*Christianity Today*, July 22, 1957, p. 39). Others, however, would hold that the church is a continuing historical society and that its authority is transmitted in orderly succession from generation to generation and that those breaking away from the ministerial succession are schismatics (see Bishop Lesslie Newbigin, *The Household of Faith*, pp. 43f, 82f). Calvin and Luther held that wherever the Gospel was truly preached and the sacraments rightly administered there was the visible church. That is, the visible church finds its continuity in the society of believers that exists throughout the centuries. Herein we have no more than stated the problem to show its difficulty of solution and different apprehensions among men.

Some would urge that we accept the episcopacy without any particular theory about it. Dr. C. C. Morrison writes, "In its famous 'Quadrilateral' proposal for church union, renewed again and again, the Anglican church asks for the acceptance only of the historic episcopate, not for the acceptance of the apostolic succession. It asks for the ministry of the united church to be ordained within this ancient succession, with the implication that respect for it, but no particular theory about it, is required" (*The Unfinished Reformation*, p. 162f). The episcopacy is to be accepted in some sort of intellectual vacuum. John Knox seeks carefully to condition the acceptance of the episcopate, "This means that the Catholic may need to make some concessions, although I believe he will find that nothing essential in Catholicism needs to be compromised. He must not insist that only sound reason for accepting episcopacy is the belief that it was the primitive church order or that Jesus or the apostles instituted it. He must not require us to believe that episcopacy constitutes the church (rather than being constituted by it or, at most, with it)—that the essence of the church consists in a priestly hierarchy, above and apart from the community rather than in the community itself, however indispensable a part of it an ordered ministry may be. He must not even demand the belief that episcopacy goes back in uninterrupted succession to the apostles, although it well may. Various particular positions on such issues must, of course, be permitted; but none must be required" (*The Early Church,* p. 145). Even with these conditions, ruled out is the "theory" that the episcopate is unscriptural. That position, seemingly, may not be permitted for it would prove divisive. It may well be that a compromise may involve all parties in greater sin than remaining in their particular denominations.

Another major obstacle in the way of organizational unity is the question of baptism. Some accept only believer's baptism and that by immersion; others believe that children have a part in the covenant and baptize infants. Both base their conviction on the authority of Scripture. For either to give up his firm conviction for the sake of organizational unity would be a greater sin than remaining in a separate denomination. But cannot each retain his belief and yet become an integral part of a unified world-church? At the most that would be a superficial unity and would invite grievous problems. Certain theological seminaries would have to remain under Baptist control. Bishops would not be free to appoint one with baptist convictions to a congregation that believed in infant baptism. Division still would remain.

The question of baptism illustrates clearly the superficiality and danger of a union based on "agreeing to disagree." Other doctrines become involved. The question of human responsibility and God's sovereign grace have separated Methodist from Presbyterian. Organizational unity would not eliminate strife between opposing camps of liberals and evangelicals, ritualists and anti-ritualists. It has been pointed out that those within the churches are scarcely aware of their denominational standards. This is attributed to modern scholarship and the modern awakening. A more realistic appraisal would attribute this ignorance to neglect of Scripture and a slumbering indifference. Within the ministry a slow awakening to the importance of theology begins to appear. The present resurgence of interest in religion may cause both minister and laymen to read the Scriptures for guidance in religious truth.

Must then the element of sin as revealed by divergent polity, doctrine, and worship remain forever within the visible church as presently constituted? Absolutely not! Paul stated to the Ephesian church that the ministry was gifted for the peculiar mission of instructing the church "till we all come in the unity of the faith, and of the knowledge of the Son of God, unto a perfect man, unto the measure of the stature of the fulness of Christ" (Eph. 4:13). The road to unity is through faith and knowledge of Christ and not through organization. As the fulness of Christ enters into the church through instruction in faith and knowledge, a glorious unity will prevail throughout the church. While the church has achieved some maturity, definite growth is still needed through the teaching ministry. Humanly speaking, centuries may pass before this unity becomes a reality. But even as the Roman Catholic Church is willing to wait centuries to accomplish her ends, so must the Protestant church be patient and yet work diligently to bring unity to fruition.

RESURGENT CONFESSIONALISM

Fear has been expressed by ecumenists that the renewed interest in the standards of denominations may scuttle the ecumenical movement. However, one blessing of the ecumenical movement is the search into the why and wherefore of denominational existence. Many have been amazed at the depth and relevance of Confessions of the church. Some have turned to Confessions because Liberalism has failed to produce a vital message and theology for the present generation. Dr. E. Theodore Bachman writes, "Tragic as were the heresy trials of 1955 and 1956, they were symptomatic of a deepening theological concern among

Lutherans. Their great lesson seemed to be that theology will have itself taken seriously, and not simply taken for granted; that the Confessions are not static compends of doctrinal propositions, but a dynamic witnessing to the living Word of God; that Lutheranism is not an organizational label, but a faith-filled life" (*Lutheran Churches of the World,* p. 176). Danger does exist that some may rest on a church creed without bringing it under constant review of Scripture. Such attitude would preclude the church from ever coming to the unity of faith. Nevertheless, the present resurgence of Confessionalism is a sign of health and will enable the church to go from strength to strength.

Much has been made of bitter rivalries and antagonism between churches by those who advocate corporate union, and apprehension has been expressed that resurgent denominationalism may accentuate this spirit. While some of this spirit exists, it has been greatly exaggerated. (It also exists between various parties within a single denomination.) Naturally, religious bodies exhibit zeal and may defend their peculiar beliefs in opposition to those who assail them. Yet acknowledgment is expressed that those who believe in the fundamentals of Christianity are one in Christ Jesus, in spite of differences.

The Church of Jesus Christ owes much of its beauty, strength, and power to denominationalism even though it is tinged with human weakness, error, and sin. To call it an evidence of apostasy and the greatest scandal of civilization is unjust and uncharitable. Such designations reveal a blindness to the true worth and blessing of denominations and show a terrible ignorance of history. Denominationalism has welded multitudes of people in identical polity, doctrine, and worship. While still far from the Scriptural ideal, yet progress has been made and will be made as soon as the church returns to the apostolic faith and renders obedience to the invisible Head, Jesus Christ.

Chapter IV

AUTHORITY OF SCRIPTURE

The evangelical can make a most effective contribution to the establishment of true unity by asserting and vindicating the authority of Scripture for faith and life. Only the acceptance of the authority of Scripture warrants hope that true union of Christendom may be accomplished. The mind of Christ concerning unity has found expression in the written Word. The authority of Holy Writ has been the rallying point for unity in the past and can again be for the present and future. Appeal to the authority of the revealed will of God was characteristic of the early church and also the church of the Reformation.

THE EARLY CHURCH

Without being questioned, the authority of the Old Testament of the Jewish church passed over, in the teaching of Jesus and the apostles, into the Christian church. Why, then, are the teachings of the prophets questioned or doubted when Jesus quoted them as authoritative? Christ answered and vanquished Satan with the authority of the written Law (Matt. 4:1-10). The Lord declared that if men will not hear Moses and the prophets and take direction from them for the way to God, neither will they receive knowledge from any other source regardless how spectacular (Luke 16:29, 31). The Saviour directed men to search the Scriptures because they testified of him (John 5:39). He told the Sadducees, sceptics of his generation, that they erred because of their ignorance of Scripture (Matt. 22:29).

As the authority of Old Testament Scripture was woven into the warp and woof of Christ's teachings, so also in the teachings of the apostles. This appears not in an isolated text here and there, but in the very heart of their writing. Notice how the apostle Paul carefully builds his doctrine of justification by faith on Old Testament revelation (Romans 4). The author of Hebrews established the priesthood of Christ on appeal to the Old Testament. In the book of Revelation the apostle John uses the images and figures of the Old Testament with a skill that can only be inspired. The early church was nurtured on the Old Testament and accepted its authority without question. This provided an important element in the unity of the first century church.

The authority of the apostles contributed greatly to the unity of the early church. Without this supervising authority the young church would undoubtedly have disintegrated from many cleavages and heresies. This authority of the apostles has been superseded by their permanent writings. In his high priestly prayer when the unity of believers rested so heavily on the heart of Jesus, he prayed, "Father, I pray not for these alone, but for them also which shall believe on me *through their word*" (John 17:20). The Lord gave the apostles a rare promise, saying, "He shall guide you into all truth,"—a word that may not be applied to others, but to the apostles exclusively (see John 14:17, 26; 15:26; 16:13).

That the apostles were to have permanent authority and influence over the church is indicated in a number of scriptural passages. Classic is Ephesians 2:20, "And are built upon the foundation of the apostles and prophets, Jesus Christ himself being the chief corner stone." In the apocalyptic vision, when the Church presents itself to view in its ideal condition as a glorious building, its walls rest on 12 foundations "and in them the names of the 12 apostles of the Lamb" (Rev. 21:14). Using another figure of speech our Lord said, "in the regeneration when the Son of man shall sit in the throne of his glory, ye also shall sit upon 12 thrones, judging the 12 tribes of Israel" (Matt. 19:28). This means that the apostles through their teachings rule the Church of God. We read in Matthew 23:2, 3, "The scribes and the Pharisees sit in Moses' seat: all therefore what-soever they bid you observe, that observe and do." Moses through the giving of the law ruled the old Israel until the coming of Christ. Now the apostles ruled the new Israel. The 12 *thrones* of the apostles take the place of Moses' seat. The faithful scribe of the new dispensation teaches and interprets the revelation given to the apostles.

Those who disparage and despise the authority of apostolic teaching actually perform a disservice to true unity. One of the causes of division and prevalence of the hundred and one sects in American life is the doubt cast on the authority and veracity of apostolic teaching. Many people who find a lack of authoritative preaching in the historical denominations have turned to sects for this missing note. By returning the apostolic note of authority into the life of denominations evangelicals will set the church on the right and most direct route to unity.

The Reformation resurrected the church from human tradition and deadness through establishing the authority of the written Word. The church owes much to the great formal principle of the Reformation that the Bible is the authoritative source of religious knowledge and the only rule of faith and life. Reliance upon the Bible as the trustworthy Word of God gave strength and power to the church and caused its reformation. Regardless how the Scriptures are mutilated by present day scholarship the fact cannot be contradicted that times of reformation and revival are contemporaneous with a high view of Scripture.

REVEALED RELIGION

Christianity has always prided itself on being the revealed religion and as such had exclusive claim on the souls of men. Man throughout history has felt his estrangement from God and in some manner has sought to placate and worship him. Neither nature nor the wisdom of man has revealed how man may please God and enjoy him. Man as sinner felt the need of being reconciled and needed knowledge of the way by which he could enter into fellowship with the living God. Special revelation was required whereby man could, with confidence, ascertain the will of God as to acceptable worship and obedience. The Judaeo-Christian religion has always claimed to be the recipient of the oracles of God. Paul stated concerning the Israelites, "to whom pertaineth the adoption, and the glory, and the covenants, and the giving of the law, and the service of God, and the promises" (Rom. 9:4). The author of Hebrews writes, "God, who at sundry times and in divers manners spake in time past unto the fathers by the prophets, hath in these last days spoken unto us by his Son" (Heb. 1:1, 2).

All that is required of man that he may please God, be accepted of him, and come to eternal enjoyment of him has been given by revelation. What is needful for faith, obedience, and eternal salvation has been revealed through the prophets, apostles, and the Lord Jesus Christ. This has been the proud boast of the Christian Church throughout the the past centuries and thoroughly justified.

Where is this revelation deposited? The historic answer has always been that the revelation of God's will has been deposited in holy Scriptures. The infallible source of the knowledge of God and his will for the church is discovered in the Bible. The whole objective special revelation given of God lies in the written Word. Objective truths that embrace all that is indispensable for salvation have been recorded and entrusted to the Church. Because it is *revelation,* the written Word possesses authority to command belief from all men.

The church banded together as a society based upon revealed truth. From the day of Pentecost she has proclaimed with great power, "Thus saith the Lord." Pagan Rome was conquered by the apostolic message of salvation. Heathen hordes were subdued by missionaries with an authoritative message from heaven. An ignorant and superstitious people were rescued from a degraded church, encrusted with human tradition, by an appeal to the written Word. And in the twentieth century the first and foremost task of the missionary is to translate the Bible so that those in darkness may have the revelation of the will and mind of the living God. Conquering and victorious Christianity has always proclaimed the message of Scriptures with faith that it is the revelation of God.

AUTHORITY OF EXPERIENCE

Those who reject the authority of Scripture and deny its uniqueness as the infallible revelation of God's mind and will for mankind, are confined to the position of giving authority to religious experience or to the position of agnosticism. If religious experience be authoritative then the ultimate judge of religious truth is man. At the most, Scripture is a reflector of human experience that is not normative for the twentieth century wherein experience takes on a different hue. The searching question comes as to whose experience is valid. Shall a survey be taken of the membership of the church to determine the authoritative message on the being of God, the divinity of Christ, and the way of salvation? Or should authoritative experience be limited to church councils, religious leaders, ecumenists, and professional theologians? What about the Roman Catholic Church—surely she makes claims for the validity of her experience and dogmas. The so-called fringe groups also speak of the validity of their ecstatic experience. Obviously those who emphasize revelation through religious experience cannot accept all such revelation as valid and authoritative.

Can one shrug off the religious experience of the evangelical? His soul rejoices in an infallible Scripture, in God-incarnate, in blood atonement, and in regeneration. If religious experience were the norm he could point to the experience of the early church fathers, to Augustine, to Luther, Calvin, Knox, Wesley, Spurgeon and a host of others. He can point to the experience of the historical denominations as expressed in the creeds. However, as Peter stated, "We have also a more sure word of prophecy; whereunto ye do well to take heed, as unto a light that shineth in a dark place, until the day dawn, and the day star arise in your hearts: knowing this first, that no prophecy of the scripture is of any private interpretation. For the prophecy came not in old time by the will of man: but holy men of God spake as they were moved by the Holy Ghost" (2 Pet. 1:19-21).

Church history testifies eloquently to the biblical teaching that man is fallible, sinful, unreliable, and prone to error. That applies to good men, religious men, churchmen. Protestants have always maintained the principle that councils of men may err and are never to be taken as infallible authority. The Lord's word to Isaiah may well be applied to all experiences of men, "To the law and to the testimony: if they speak not according to this word, it is because there is no light in them."

TESTIMONY OF THE SPIRIT

While the church throughout the centuries has clearly asserted that the Scriptures are the sole authoritative source of religious knowledge, she has also indicated that the supernatural light of grace wrought by the Holy Spirit is necessary for saving perception and understanding of the mind of God in the Scriptures. Calvin was one of the first to indicate the teaching of Scripture that only in conjunction of the Word and the Spirit can sinful man obtain a gracious, saving, spiritual perception of revealed truth. This is called the testimony of the Holy Spirit. Not the testimony of human consciousness, not the testimony of Christian scholars, not even the testimony of the visible church—but the testimony of the Holy Spirit gives assurance to the believer that Scripture is the very Word of God. The Holy Spirit may use means to bring about this confidence and assurance but he is the ultimate source.

The incident of Christ and the two disciples on the way to Emmaus illustrates the function of the Holy Spirit (Luke 24). Christ rebuked the two for their slowness of heart to believe all that the prophets have spoken. Beginning with Moses and all the prophets, he expounded the Scriptures concerning himself. They testified, "Did not our hearts burn within us, while he talked with us by the way, and while he opened to us the scriptures?" Christ confirmed that the Old Testament was an authentic revelation of himself, but that the understanding of man needed to be opened before he could grasp the recorded objective truths. Paul echoed that fact: "Now we have received, not the spirit of the world, but the spirit which is of God; that we might know the things that are freely given to us of God" (1 Cor. 2:12).

Spiritual ignorance and darkness of man requires the operation of the Holy Spirit before revealed truth can be grasped. The Scriptures reveal the way to reconciliation to God with clear light. But light avails nothing to one that is born blind. The Spirit gives to darkened souls eyes to behold the marvelous light of the Gospel.

Some would consider it derogatory to the Spirit to limit him to confirming and interpreting the written Word. (We write now of his relation to revelation and not other functions such as sanctifying, comforting, and guiding.) The holy Scriptures, however, are the product of the Spirit who inspired men to write what God wanted recorded. More derogatory to the Spirit is to attribute to him the varied and contradictory religious experiences which do not conform to Scripture. The confusion of Babel must not be made his responsibility.

SCRIPTURE AND UNITY

Physician heal thyself has been the charge levelled at those who hold to the authority and inspiration of Scripture. Why do divisions multiply among those who hold to the verbal inspiration of the Word? With one infallible source for faith and life, why does "biblicism" produce so many independent churches? Why does concern for Christian unity press so heavily on the hearts of those who have a low view of Scripture and receive such scant attention from those who have a high view of the Bible? These questions will be more fully discussed in the chapter on "Evangelical Disunity." Meanwhile, whatever defect may be found in evangelicals let it not be imputed to some imperfection of Scripture. The written Word rightly understood and interpreted will produce that type of unity for which Christ prayed.

The creeds of historical denominations are evangelical in character. Unfortunately the past several generations have not been properly indoctrinated through the exposition of the creeds and the Scriptures upon which they are founded. Lack of biblical preaching has caused a famine within the denominations, and hungry hearts by the thousands have turned to movements where the bread of God's Word is provided. Distressing experiences within the denominations have caused many people to look upon them with distrust and suspicion. They feel that they can protect the heritage of the Gospel better within an independent framework. Emphasis on separation and individualism have precluded them from forming strong denominations. Preoccupation with the milk of the Word has prevented them from partaking of the meat of the Word; especially is this true in respect to the biblical teaching of the nature of the Church. Given time, these movements may develop into powerful, influential, and healthy denominations. Far be it for historical denominations to cast stones of criticism upon them, for the cause of their existence finds its root in the denominations themselves.

But are not the divisions among evangelicals a stumbling block to those who would come to Christ? To what group can they turn for truth of salvation? Chrysostom gives an effective answer. He wrote, "What shall we say unto the Gentiles? A Gentile cometh and saith, 'I would be a Christian, but I know not unto whom amongst you I should adhere. There are many contentions, seditions, and tumults amongst you: what opinion to choose I know not. Everyone says, I am in the truth, whom shall I believe? I am utterly ignorant of what is in the Scripture about these things.'" Here is the answer of Chrysostom, "This makes wholly for us; for if we should say that we believe on probable reasonings, thou mayst justly be troubled; but seeing we profess that we believe in the Scriptures, which are plain and true, it is easy for thee to judge and determine. He that yields his consent unto them, he is a Christian; and he that contends against them is far from the rule of Christianity" (*Homil.* 33, *in act. Apost.* cap. xv.) The evangelical points away from himself to the written Word and to the living Word revealed through it.

The fault for disunity does not lie in Scriptures. When men obtain deeper apprehension of its revealed truth, unity will become more and more evident. A keen analysis of the situation of the present day will reveal that disunity is not caused by the teachings of the Bible, but the groundless imposition of things necessary to be believed and practices beyond Scripture warrant. The additions and traditions of men are the sources of differences among Christians.

TESTIMONY OF THE CREEDS

Some ecumenists show alarm at the present trend towards appreciation of the Confessions of the Church. They fear that the resurgence of interest in creeds will scuttle the projected world-church. Examination of creedal statements will reveal that they uphold the inspiration and authority of Scripture. A few examples will suffice.

The Lutheran Formula of Concord (1576)

> We believe, confess, and teach that the only rule and
> norm, according to which all dogmas and all doctors ought

to be esteemed and judged, is no other whatever than the prophetic and apostolic writings both of the Old and of the New Testament.

The French Confession of Faith (1559)

We believe that the Word contained in these books has proceeded from God, and receives its authority from him alone, and not from men. And inasmuch as it is the rule of all truth, containing all that is necessary for the service of God and for our salvation, it is not lawful for men, nor even angels, to add to it, to take away from it, or to change it. Whence it follows that no authority, whether of antiquity, or custom, or numbers, or edicts, or decrees, or councils, or visions, or miracles, should be opposed to these Holy Scriptures, but, on the contrary, all things should be examined, regulated, and reformed according to them.

The Belgic Confession (1561)

We believe that these Holy Scriptures fully contain the will of God, and that whatsoever man ought to believe unto salvation, is sufficiently taught therein. . . . Therefore we reject with all our hearts whatsoever doth not agree with this infallible rule, which the Apostles have taught us, saying, *Try the spirits whether they are of God;* likewise, *If there come any unto you, and bring not this doctrine, receive him not into your house.*

The Scotch Confession of Faith (1560)

As we believe and confess the Scriptures of God sufficient to instruct and make the man of God perfect, so do we affirm and avow the authority of the same to be of God, and neither to depend on men nor angels. We affirm, therefore, that such as allege the Scripture to have no other authority but that which it has received from the Kirk, to be blasphemous against God, and injurious to the true Kirk, which always hears and obeys the voice of her own Spouse and Pastor; but take not upon her to be mistress over the same.

The Thirty-nine Articles of the Church of England (1562)

Holy Scripture containeth all things necessary to salvation: so that whatsoever is not read therein, nor may be proved therein, nor may be proved thereby, is not required of any man, that it should be believed as an article of the Faith, or be thought requisite or necessary to salvation. In the name of the Holy Scripture we do understand those canonical Books of the Old and New Testament, of whose authority was never any doubt in the Church.

The Westminster Confession of Faith (1647)

. . . . therefore it pleased the Lord, at sundry times, and in divers manners, to reveal himself, and to declare that his will unto his Church; and afterwards, for the better preserving and propagating of the truth, and for the more sure establishment and comfort of the Church against the corruption of the flesh, and the malice of Satan and of the world, to commit the same wholly unto writing; which maketh the holy Scripture to be most necessary; those former ways of God's revealing his will unto his people being now ceased. Under the name of holy Scripture, or the Word of God written, are now contained all the Books of the Old and New Testament. . . . All which are given by inspiration of God, to be the rule of faith and life."

The New Hampshire Baptist Confession (1833)

We believe that the Holy Bible was written by men divinely inspired, and is a perfect treasure of heavenly instruction; that it has God for its author, salvation for its end, and truth without any mixture of error for its matter; that it reveals the principles by which God will judge us; and therefore is, and shall remain to the end of the world, the true center of Christian union, and the supreme standard by which all human conduct, creeds, and opinions should be tried.

As far as we know, no denomination has repudiated its historic creed or revised its statement on the authority of Scriptures. Many feel that Higher Criticism has destroyed confidence in the trustworthiness of Scripture. One must discern, however, between the objective facts discovered by that biblical science and the subjective reasoning of its scholars. One really assured conclusion can be made as one studies the history of Higher Criticism—the "assured results" of the past generation become the "discarded results" of the next generation. This science evidently is in a major transition at the present time in regard to the dating of documents with the trend towards earlier dating. The evangelical has nothing to fear of Higher Criticism except to be grieved that this biblical science has caused many to reject the testimony of the creeds to the trustworthiness and authority of Holy Writ.

CURRENT MISUNDERSTANDINGS

As criticism of the evangelical's position on Scripture is studied, one becomes aware of caricature rather than sympathetic understanding and realistic appraisal. Men of straw are conjured and belabored. One common accusation levelled against those who believe in the plenary inspiration of the Word is that they worship a book rather than the living Lord. The evangelical, however, testifies with the Psalmist, "O how love I thy law! it is my meditation all the day"; "More to be desired are they than gold, yea, than much fine gold: sweeter also than honey and the honeycomb" (Ps. 119:97; 19:10). Because the Bible reveals the living Saviour, the believer rejoices and delights in the written Word. Whatever revelation we possess of Christ comes to us through the Old and New Testaments. Even the most radical critic is indebted to Scripture for the few scraps of revelation he desires to retain.

Another man of straw pictures the evangelical as maintaining that all sentiments contained in Scripture are authoritative because written in the Word. Simple inclusion of a statement in Scripture does not make it authoritative as it may have been uttered by a demon or a wicked man. Dr. John Dick made this sagacious statement, "From the mere admission of any fact into the inspired history, no other conclusion can be warrantably drawn, than that it actually took place, and it was the will of God that we should be acquainted with it: its moral nature, its conformity or disconformity to the standard of truth and rectitude, must be ascertained by some other test than its simple insertion in the Bible. Were clear ideas formed on this subject, some misapplications of passages would be prevented, and some objections which are brought against the inspiration of the sacred books, would either be not advanced at all, or would be immediately perceived to be inconclusive or unjust. . . . Whether the conduct related be wise or foolish, moral or immoral, we must determine by the judgment pronounced in the Scriptures themselves on particular cases, or by applying those principles and general rules, which are laid down in them to regulate our decisions" (*Lectures On Theology*, pp. 118, 119).

The dictation theory of inspiration also is attributed to the evangelical. Every word in the sacred books has been supposed to be immediately dictated to the minds of writers. However, evangelicals have always maintained that inspiration does not supersede the use of natural faculties and the use of source documents as is evidenced in Scripture itself. However, many things could not be known by natural means and can only be attributed to direct communication from God. No iron curtain exists between earth and heaven to prevent revelation.

Both through the subjectivism of the higher critics and misunderstanding of the doctrine of plenary inspiration, the Scriptures have been neglected as the source of unity in faith and action. The evangelical may have a hard task of convincing biased and prejudiced preachers and theologians as to the trustworthiness of the written Word, nevertheless that is his duty and responsibility. The study of biblical theology will do much to establish the unity of the sacred books and reveal their divine inspiration. However, the use of all biblical sciences—textual criticism, hermeneutics, biblical and systematic theology, etc., —should be employed by evangelical scholars to vindicate the authority of Scriptures. In so doing a real contribution will be made to the unity of the Christian church.

Chapter V

THAT THEY MAY BE ONE

Many deprecate the doctrine of verbal inspiration with such descriptive words as biblicism, obscurantism, and literalism. However, when it comes to one sentence in the seventeenth chapter of the Gospel of St. John even the most radical and liberal ecumenist becomes guilty of a literalistic interpretation of which no evangelical has been guilty. While the question of dating may have bearing on the reliability of statements attributed to Jesus as asserted by liberal scholars, of this sentence there seems to be no question of validity. With all pontifical authority and with a dogmatism that tolerates no contrary opinion, the often quoted sentence is pronounced to be the very inspired Word of God and true revelation of the mind of Christ. The sentence appears as a petition uttered by Christ in his high priestly prayer, "That they all may be one, as thou, Father, art in me, and I in thee, that they also may be one in us; that the world may believe that thou hast sent me" (John 17:21). This petition of our Lord has become the charter of the ecumenical movement and finds constant repetition in all its literature.

It has been assumed that the earnest appeal of Christ, made in the shadow of Gethsemane and Calvary, pleads for corporate church union. Such assumption pays scant attention to the true meaning of the petition.

VISIBLE CHURCH UNITY

Christ's supplication, without a doubt, does press for visible church unity. Without a visible oneness how could the burden

41

of the petition be effected, "that the world may believe that thou hast sent me"? The world cannot behold the invisible. Surely the world would be more inclined to believe the divine mission of Christ if unity among professing Christians were perceptible. Christendom split into fragments must puzzle the unregenerate world and cause it to doubt the value of Christ's entrance into history. The church united in faith, love, worship and purpose would not fail to impress the world and cause respect for her Leader.

Those who would belittle church unity must quarrel with the petition of Christ. He definitely prays the Father to establish a visible unity among his followers that the world may believe in his mission. While recognizing this need the evangelical, however, is distressed that many ecumenists pay scant attention to the type of church unity for which Christ pleads. In spite of the definitional clause in the petition the ecumenist envisions his type of union—a single comprehensive organization with some acceptable government whether congregational, presbyterian or episcopal. Was this ecumenical church in the mind of Christ as he petitioned the Father?

Our Lord defined the unity he desired with the clause, "as thou, Father, art in me, and I in thee." The particle *as* cannot be ignored if one would interpret the mind of Christ. The concord that exists between the Father and the Son forms the pattern of unity for which the church must strive.

ONE IN DOCTRINE

Obviously, harmony exists between the Father and the Son in regard to doctrine. Jesus insisted that his teachings were in agreement with the Father. "My doctrine is not mine, but his that sent me," he claimed in John 7:16. He said further, "I speak to the world those things which I have heard of him. . . . I do nothing of myself; but as my Father hath taught me" (John 8:26, 28). Again he said, "For I have not spoken of myself, but the Father which sent me, he gave me a commandment, what I should say, and what I should speak" (John 12:49). These are but a few passages in which Jesus strongly maintains that his doctrine is identical with that of the Father. Unity with contradictions in doctrine was not the burden of the high priestly prayer.

Impatient designers of the ecumenical church shudder at the thought of doctrinal unity, which either appears unimportant or impossible of achievement. Fear has been expressed that doctrinal emphasis will scuttle the ecumenical movement. Yet how can two walk together except they be agreed? Since Jesus stressed doctrinal agreement between the Father and himself, how can any movement worthy of his name ignore this important cohesive force? Organizational union without concord in doctrine will fail to impress the observant world. Actually, doctrinal unity is an important ingredient of the mortar which will hold together the living stones of the Temple of God.

ONE IN PURPOSE

Between the Father and the Son there was mutual agreement in the carrying on of the work of redemption. They were one in purpose. Jesus said, "For I came down from heaven, not to do mine own will, but the will of him that sent me. . . . And this is the will of him that sent me, that everyone which seeth the Son, and believeth on him, may have everlasting life" (John 6:38, 40). The will of the Father was the salvation of his people through the atoning work of Christ upon the cross. Thus Jesus could say in anticipation of Calvary, "I have finished the work which thou gavest me to do" (John 17:4).

The church must echo that agreement of purpose by proclaiming the message of redemption to every creature. Salvation of the lost was the purpose for which God sent his Son into the world. In fulfilling this mission the Church comes into the unity of the Father and the Son. The rapid growth of the first-century church can in part be ascribed to the unity manifested by believers in proclaiming the message of redemption. Organizational unity, where the one purpose of proclaiming redemption does not exist, will fail to impress the unbelieving world.

ONE IN LOVE

The pagan world stood amazed at the demonstration of love in the lives of believers. "How these Christians love one another. They are even ready to die for each other," was the discerning remark of a pagan. The church is described as being of one heart and of one soul in Acts 4:32. What affected one affected all. With surprise and admiration the first-century world beheld a fellowship bound by love, embracing men of every race and language. This was the visible unity for which Jesus prayed and which astonished the world.

The present ecumenical movement can never succeed until the desire for closer union springs from dynamic love in the hearts of church members. Many are enamored of ecumenity because a comprehensive organization seems more efficient and more economical. Many are impressed because church leaders stress its importance. However, a unity brought about by economic reasons or by ecclesiastical pressure has no resemblance to unity engendered by love. A unity built upon superficial motives has little resemblance to the unity of heart and soul of the early church. Nor is it the unity for which Jesus prayed.

INVISIBLE

How one can argue for visible unity in organizational form from the union existing in the Godhead is difficult to conceive. Does the Godhead form a corporate unity that can be seen? Does the Divine unity make impression upon the physical senses? Does the Triune God manifest himself in material essence before the concord subsisting between the Father, Son, and Holy Spirit can be believed? What a crass, carnal, literalistic, and materializing sense this makes of our Lord's petition.

 In the Old Testament dispensation a lower physical representation of spiritual truths was needed for the church in an infant state. A material altar, material sacrifice and material temple spelled out significant and saving truths. The Israelites showed their lack of spirituality when they demanded a king whom they could see. They were not content with the rule of the King in heaven whom they could not behold with their physical eyes. Their constant sin was the desire for material gods whom they could touch and grasp. In consideration of their infancy, God in his mercy revealed spiritual truths through the means of material types.

However, the new dispensation was placed on a higher plane. The church obtained adulthood and put away childish things. She was ready to worship without material aids and serve the King reigning in heaven. Jesus intimated this in John 4:21, 23, "Woman, believe me, the hour cometh, when ye shall neither in this mountain, nor yet at Jerusalem, worship the Father. . . . But the hour cometh, and now is, when the true worshippers shall worship the Father in spirit and in truth: for the Father seeketh such to worship him." The time had come to dispense with visible and material aids in worship.

Those who express impatience with the concept of the invisible Church and with spiritual unity surely forget that the new dispensation has been raised to a higher spiritual plane. "In spirit and in truth" elevates the church from the material and types. The advocates of making an impact upon the world with a visible organization depart from the high plane of New Testament revelation. The preaching of truth with the power of the Holy Spirit will change the world. When one understands and grasps the spiritual emphasis of New Testament revelation he will not interpret the Lord's supplication in his high priestly prayer for a mere visible organization of churches. The Lord's prayer for unity has greater depth.

UNITY OF EARLY CHURCH

No one will seriously argue that there has been a complete fulfillment of the Lord's petition in history. Nevertheless, the first-century church does reflect a great unity of doctrine, faith, life, and purpose. The Epistles reveal the struggle of the church to achieve the type of unity for which Christ prayed. For instance, the epistle to the Galatians shows how Paul withstood the infiltration of false doctrine lest it split the church. Further, in Ephesians 4:11-14 he emphasized that the work of the ministry was to bring the Church "in the unity of the faith, and of the knowledge of the Son of God, unto a perfect man, unto the measure of the stature of the fulness of Christ: that we henceforth be no more children, tossed to and fro, and carried about with every wind of doctrine." Faith and knowledge that has the Son of God as the object will bring about genuine unity —a unity that can be destroyed only by heresy.

CENTRAL CONTROL

Recent writers have despaired of finding a pattern for their conception of the ecumenical church in the New Testament. John Knox writes, "Our recognition of the fact that the church, which has never been fully united in a visible unity, was not thus united in the Apostolic Age, will keep us from interpreting the goal of the ecumenical movement as being simply the restoration of the forms and usages of the early church" (*The Early Church and the Coming Great Church,* p. 15). He maintains also that "There was no one over-all organization and no central control" (*ibid.,* p. 43); and "There was no single comprehensive organization of the churches nor can a universal pattern of organization be traced among all the churches severally" (*ibid.,* p. 83).

Under no condition can the Lord's petition, "that they may be one," be interpreted as a prayer for "one over-all organization under central control" or for, "a single comprehensive organization of the churches." Our Lord first of all prayed for unity among his individual disciples (John 17:11). Subsequent history reveals that this petition was sorely needed and also reveals that the supplication was answered. After praying for unity of the apostles the Saviour pleaded for unity among all those who would believe in him upon the word of the disciples (John 17:21). The unification of organized churches does not form the burden of the petitions. In Revelation 2 and 3 where our Lord is depicted as giving admonition to the seven churches there is no hint that the great failure of the churches was in the lack of organizational unity. They were rebuked for losing their first love, for coldness in service, for toleration of heresy, and for failure to exercise discipline. These were the sins against unity. Not one hint of criticism appears for the existence of separate organizations.

The absence of "central control" is explained by the consciousness of the New Testament church that the headship of Christ was a living and vital reality. Expression of that fact is found in Colossians 2:19: "And not holding the Head, from which the body by joints and bands having nourishment ministered and knit together increaseth with the increase of God." Here is true organic unity—a spiritual unity which may disappoint those who feel that visible organizational unity is the high goal of ecumenity. The New Testament, however, emphasizes the spiritual Headship of Christ and the spiritual unity of believers.

Visible unity of the church is the desperate need of the present day. Its absence harms the cause of Christianity. Yet the only effectual unity is the unity for which Christ prayed and which the New Testament Church illustrated. The Church today must not yield to the temptation of searching for a more human and a lower pattern for the sake of immediate achievement. There must be no bypassing of the pattern of unity expressed in the Lord's petition, "as thou, Father, art in me, and I in thee," and the pattern of unity exemplified by the early church. While this spiritual unity may take longer to achieve, it is that for which our Lord prayed.

Chapter VI

UNITY OF THE SPIRIT

The indwelling Holy Spirit secures the unity of the Church. Establishing and strengthening unity among the people of God falls within the province of the third person of the Holy Trinity. The early church experienced an earnest of unity on the day of Pentecost when representatives from every nation cried out in amazement, "How hear we in our own language the wonderful works of God?" The tower of Babel—the man-made attempt at unity—brought forth division and confusion of tongues. The outpouring of the Holy Spirit on Pentecost brought forth a universal spiritual language that could be understood by all nationalities and would bind together the children of God from every nation. In every language, people would understand the mighty works of God: calvary, resurrection, regeneration, justification, reconciliation, sanctification, eternal life, and joy. The unity introduced at Pentecost was a foreshadowing of the future unity that would characterize the church under the power of the Holy Spirit.

The apostle Paul was conscious of that unity and strongly urged Ephesian Christians to maintain the unity of the Spirit (Eph. 4:3). A sad commentary on the ecclesiastical world of today is the necessity of asserting that the Spirit mentioned is none other than the third person of the Trinity. The person of the Spirit is obscured and sometimes equated with new life and new love brought in to the community. The fruit activated by the Spirit does not form the Spirit. The tendency to confound human consciousness with the Spirit must be resisted. Nor should it be thought that virtue and power emanating from God constitute the Holy Spirit. Unfortunately, the unitarian concept of the Godhead is gaining ground in some denominations that were historically trinitarian. However, none other than the third person of the Trinity broods over the new creation to bring forth the beauty of unity even as he brought order and beauty out of what was waste and void in the old creation.

The glorious unity engendered by the Holy Spirit was dramatically illustrated on the day of Pentecost when from a mixture of nationalities the Christian church became visible. Three thousand souls were welded together and continued steadfastly in the apostles' doctrine and fellowship, and in breaking of bread and in prayers (Acts 2:41, 42). The immediate effect of this outpouring of the Spirit was a unity of doctrine and spiritual fellowship. Similarity of belief and gathering together for prayer gave visibility to the early church and demonstrated unity of the Spirit. The union of Christians in doctrine and their association in the breaking of bread and in prayer followed the indwelling of the Holy Spirit. Identity of faith, of love, of hope, of desires characterize those moved by the third person of the Trinity.

The apostle Paul presupposes the existence of unity such as that demonstrated on Pentecost when he warns the church at Ephesus to make real effort to maintain this quality—"Endeavoring to keep the unity of the Spirit in the bond of peace" (Eph. 4:3). The import of his warning must not be misunderstood to mean that unity is the product of peace or simply consists of peace. The existence of peace among the people of God reveals the presence of the Spirit and indicates his activity. Peace gives visibility to the inward unity created by the Spirit. Lack of tranquility indicates the absence of the Holy Spirit.

VITAL BOND

Being a citizen of a particular nation brings about a feeling of kinship with fellow citizens. Belonging to one ecclesiastical structure may also create a sense of affinity. However, God designed a deeper and more vital bond for the Christian. Through the Holy Spirit the believer enters into close relation to the Lord Jesus Christ. This common relationship, formed by the Spirit, gives to believers a sense of unity stronger than that brought about by a common citizenship or by church membership. Living relationship to Christ with the consequent sense of fellowship, is authored by the Holy Spirit. In this the unity of the Spirit consists, and of infinitely more value than organizational bonds.

Mere citizenship in a nation or membership in a church does not in itself cause a feeling of kindness and love that must prevail if harmony is to be achieved. Disruptive evil forces exist in both nation and church. Hatred, envy, greed and kindred sins induce friction and separation in family, nation and church. Human beings in their own strength have failed to remove divisive evils from society. Supernatural power alone can change human dispositions from evil to good. The Holy Spirit provides a sanctifying influence that removes evil and implants good and thereby establishes concord.

Among sinful lusts mentioned by Paul in the fifth chapter of Galatians are enmities, strife, jealousies, wraths, factions, divisions and envyings. These vanquish harmony and peace. Belonging to one particular church or denomination does not remove evils that cause dissension and discord. Every pastor knows the grievous trouble that the sins enumerated by Paul stir up within the congregation and the scandal they cause to the outsider. The unregenerate man does not as a rule become disturbed by the many denominations within the nation but does become troubled by factions and fightings within the local congregation. That is his point of contact. Divisive evils that cause scandal to the outsider can be removed only by the Holy Spirit. Those who walk in the Spirit will not fulfill the lusts of the flesh. Unity cannot exist without the sanctifying influence of the Holy Spirit. More zeal in prayer for the presence of the Holy Spirit would accomplish more towards the establishment of concord and harmony among Christians than efforts spent in removing denominational fences.

Implanting positive virtues as well as removing evils fall in the province of the third person of the Trinity and is essential to concord. The fruit of the Spirit, Paul informs us in the fifth chapter of Galatians, is love, joy, peace, long-suffering, kindness, goodness, faithfulness, meekness and self-control. Without these virtues one may succeed in building a structure stone upon stone but without mortar to cement it together into a solid whole. Organizational visibility occupies the mind of ecumenists, but what can show forth greater visibility than the manifestation throughout the entire church of love, joy and peace? The early church was made perceptible to the pagan world by the love and serenity of Christians. The twentieth century cannot fail to be more impressed by a tangible evidence of love, joy, and peace than by an efficient and centrally controlled organization. Holiness more than outward solidarity impresses the worldly mind. This type of visible unity depends entirely upon the indwelling of the Holy Spirit.

UNITY OF FAITH AND KNOWLEDGE

The Spirit also promotes unity by gifts with which he endows the church. Both in the twelfth chapter of First Corinthians and the fourth chapter of Ephesians attention is drawn to the diversity of gifts bestowed by the same Spirit. The grand purpose of these gifts was "For the perfecting of the saints, unto the work of ministering, unto the building up of the body of Christ: till we all attain unto the unity of faith and knowledge of the Son of God" (Eph. 4:12, 13). The New Testament stresses the importance of the unity of faith and knowledge while remaining almost silent with regard to unity of structure and organization that looms so large in the minds of some ecumenists.

Contrary to opinion, the world is not so perplexed and puzzled by duplication of organizations as by conflicting voices emanating from various groups within the visible church. Who is teaching the truth? is the question frequently asked. The disastrous impact of contradictory doctrines does more to destroy the appearance of unity than the lack of centrally controlled organization. The Spirit goes to the heart of the matter by endowing the ministry with gifts to bring forth unity of the faith and the knowledge of the Son of God. Unity authored by the Spirit becomes visible in identity of faith and knowledge among believers.

To communicate faith and knowledge the Holy Spirit employs the written Word. The modern (yet old) attempt to detach the Spirit from the written revelation has done untold harm to the unity of the church. P. T. Forsyth wrote, "Detached from the Word, the supernatural action of the Holy Spirit becomes gradually the natural evolution of the human spirit. The Spirit becomes identified with the natural humanity" (*Faith, Freedom, and the Future,* p. 95). The religious experience of a generation becomes identified with the spirit. Yet the experience of one generation may differ and even contradict the experience of another generation. Thus the Spirit is saddled with the responsibility of contradiction and confusion. Religious experience that differs from the revelation given through the prophets and apostles cannot be regarded as true and authentic. The Spirit does not teach a faith and knowledge in contradiction to the written Word which he inspired.

The thrust of the Ephesian passage (4:11-13) indicates that the Holy Spirit endowed the Church with the ministry for the purpose of causing all to come into the unity of the faith and of the knowledge of the Son of God. Jesus Christ is the object of faith and the content of knowledge. The unity of faith means that all shall possess the same confidence in the divine Son of God as Saviour and Lord. The ministry, called and gifted by the Spirit, declares that faith which lays hold of Christ unto eternal life. The unity of knowledge means that all be informed of the facts relating to Christ. Such knowledge includes the pre-existence, incarnation, earthly life and ministry, crucifixion, resurrection, ascension, present reign and coming again of the Messiah. It includes also the interpretation of these events as given by the inspired writers of the Scriptures. Only as the ministry labors to instruct believers in the faith and knowledge of the Son of God does it fufill the mission to which it has been called and enriched by the Holy Spirit.

SEEKING THE SPIRIT

The Church must learn how to open her heart to the sweet influences of the third person of the Trinity that spiritual unity may prevail. The Holy Spirit may be grieved, offended, and quenched. More than a passive attitude is required to attract the indwelling of the Spirit. Heart searching and supplication are positive requirements that demand activity on the part of the church. Whatever offends must be eradicated and the Spirit's presence implored. A church solicitous to please the Spirit is a church active in true ecumenity.

The evangelical more than any other understands the nature and quality of spiritual unity. He sees the fallacy and shallowness of an ecumenity that would achieve unity through a central organization. This increases his responsibility and rebukes him for the lack of spiritual unity evidenced by those who hold to evangelical Christianity. He comes far short of that perfect man and the measure of the stature of the fullness of Christ (Eph. 4:13). He must admonish false ecumenity not only with his lips but by a display of true unity among the brethren. Love and peace are as visible as concrete and stone. The evangelical will not prevail in rebuking the error of some aspects of the modern ecumenical movement until the unity of the Spirit prevails in his midst.

Chapter VII

IN CHRIST

What the ecumenical movement will do with Jesus Christ remains the greatest concern of the evangelical. Attention has been drawn in Chapter II to the various conceptions of Christ prevalent in the theological world of today. This does not seem to distress those who are occupied in achieving organizational unity. The ecumenical movement seems broad enough to include a number of "Christs," yet unity must be accomplished "in Christ" as we are informed repeatedly. One cannot be blamed for being somewhat puzzled and bewildered as he seeks to discern the nature of unity in Christ when different "Christs" confront him.

Others have perceived that the Christ of the ecumenical movement may be one different than the Christ of Matthew, Mark, Luke, and John. Dr. Marion John Bradshaw, professor of the philosophy of religion at Bangor Theological Seminary, makes that observation in his book, *Free Churches and Christian Unity*. No one would accuse him of being a "fundamentalist." He writes, "It is evident that in much they say of 'Christ,' the ecumenists do not mean the person whose words and deeds are recorded in the New Testament books called the Gospels," and "It is not the real Jesus, but a synthetic or even mythical figure, about whom the seeming or real totalitarianism of the ecumenical movement is being developed" (pp. 67, 72). Dr. Bradshaw attacks the World Council of Churches' formula,

"Our Lord Jesus Christ as God and Saviour," as being too exclusive and unbiblical.

Equally bewildering and puzzling is the authoritative and full knowledge of the "mind of Christ" that appears constantly in ecumenical literature. With rigid dogmatism (so despised in the evangelical) the assertion is made that the mind of Christ reveals the absolute necessity of forming a world-wide church under one organization. A new authority has arisen—apparently not the Jesus Christ of the Gospels—a Christ who emerges in the experience and consciousness of the ecumenical movement. The revelation of the mind of this new Christ has somehow escaped the notice of evangelicals and some ecumenists who do not acknowledge a directive from Christ to form one church structure. This Christ must exclude some from the revelation of his mind.

CHRIST OF THE EVANGELICAL

The evangelical discovers the source of knowledge of Christ in the Old and New Testaments, both of which reveal the person and work of the Messiah. Where else can one find knowledge of Christ? Is not the prophesied Messiah, the historical Christ, and the Christ of experience one and the same? Would one quarrel with the assertion of the Epistle to the Hebrews that Jesus Christ is the same yesterday, and today, and forever? The term *Christ* and other theological terminology are wrested by radical liberal theologians from the Scriptures. They seek to satisfy their hunger and that of others with some chosen crumbs from the table of God's Word. The Christian, however, is satisfied with nothing less than the Bread of life, Christ Jesus, revealed in Scripture. The written Word points him to the living Word whom he adores and worships.

Because the early church discerned the importance of a proper and true conception of the person of Christ, she concerned herself immediately with Christology. The first fifteen hundred years produced four Symbols—Apostles, Nicene, Athanasian, and Chalcedon. With the possible exception of the Apostles' Creed, they were concerned with the doctrine of the Trinity in relation to Christ. Though the bitter controversy caused many heartaches and made a spectacle to the world, it attributed to the doctrine of the one and undivided person of Christ that unified the thought of Christian churches to this day. Although the Roman Catholic Church has defected from many cardinal doctrines of the Word, she remains faithful to the doctrine of the Trinity and the person of Christ. (She, of course, endangers her orthodox position by unscriptural dogmas concerning Mary.) Ecumenists may be well advised to make the Chalcedon doctrine of Christ the starting point of the ecumenical movement since history proves its unifying influence.

The Chalcedon Symbol defines the person of Christ as follows:

> We, then, following the holy Fathers, all with one consent, teach men to confess one and the same Son, our Lord Jesus Christ, the same perfect in Godhead and also perfect in manhood; truly God and truly man, of a reasonable (rational) soul and body; consubstantial (co-essential) with the Father according to the Godhead, and consubstantial with us according to the Manhood; in all things like unto us, without sin; begotten before all ages of the Father according to the Godhead, and in these latter days, for us and for our salvation, born of the Virgin Mary, the Mother of God, according to the Manhood; one and the same Christ, Son, Lord, Only-begotten, to be acknowledged in two natures, inconfusedly, unchangeably, indivisibly, inseparably; the distinction of natures being by no means taken away by the union, but rather the property of each nature being preserved, and concurring in one Person and one Subsistence, not parted or divided into two persons, but one and the same Son, and only begotten, God the Word, the Lord Jesus Christ; as the prophets from the beginning (have declared) concerning him, and the Lord Jesus Christ himself has taught us, and the Creed of the holy Fathers has handed down to us.

Chalcedonian Christology, one may observe, is a complete synthesis of scriptural teaching on the person of the Lord. The formulation came about through the faith of a large body of Christian men during the course of a century. Who can measure the prayers, the zeal, the tears, the efforts of God-fearing men in bringing forth this noble Confession that has found acceptance in all the major creeds of the church? That the twentieth century must wage battle over the doctrine of the person of Christ seems a terrible tragedy in light of what has been accomplished.

Acceptance of the Chalcedonian Christology would spare the church from modern (though ancient) errors of which the Tillichian heresy is an example in that he maintains that Jesus became God. Shedd in his *History of Christ Doctrine* writes, "Another important implication in the Chalcedon Christology is that it is the Divinity, and not the humanity, which constitutes the root and basis of Christ's personality. The incarnation is the humanizing of deity, and not the deification of humanity. The second subsistence in the Divine Essence assumes human nature to itself; so that it is the Godhood, and not the manhood, which is prior and determining in the new complex-person that results. The redemption of mankind is accomplished, not by the elevation of the finite to the infinite, but by the humiliation of the infinite to the finite." Tillich's conception of Christ sets the church back some fifteen hundred years.

The admonition of the author of the Epistle to the Hebrews may well be taken to heart by this present generation in regard to the person of Christ, "Of whom we have many things to say, and hard to be uttered, seeing ye are dull of hearing. For when for the time ye ought to be teachers, ye have need that one teach you again which be the first principles of the oracles of God; and are become such as have need of milk, and not of strong meat." For the church to begin anew with the formulation of the doctrine of Christ is to go back to childhood and even infancy. Just to give a hazy indefinite picture of Christ is the church's shame and not her glory. The church should start with Chalcedonian Christology and build thereon if more light comes from the Word or if the doctrine can be stated more clearly and effectively.

FEDERAL HEAD

So much stress has been placed on the phrase "in Christ" as indicative of responsibility to be one in visible organization that the basic scriptural significance of the expression has been lost sight of and forgotten. The fundamental purpose is to reveal existence of a new creation, a new race, a new humanity, a new community—that has become so by virtue of being in Christ. Before the Fall man was under a covenant of works, wherein God promised him (through Adam, the federal head of the race) eternal blessedness if he perfectly kept the law. Through the disobedience of the federal head, Adam, the creation was cursed, the race fell, humanity suffered, and the community became disrupted. Through the obedience of the new federal head, the second Adam, a new and blessed creation came into being, a new race was lifted up, a new humanity received healing, and a new community experienced unity and harmony. The old covenant of works was displaced by the new covenant of grace.

The representation of Adam and of Christ is stated succinctly in Scripture, "For as in Adam all die, even so in Christ shall all be made alive" (I Cor. 15:22). The federal headship of both Adam and Christ is developed more fully in Romans 5:12-21. The passage declares that by one man sin entered into the world and death passed upon all men. But if through the offence of one many be dead much more the grace of God abounded unto many through Christ Jesus. And verse 19 of the passage states, "For as by one man's disobedience many were made sinners, so by the obedience of one shall many be made righteous." The blessed result of Christ's obedience unto death is summed up in the glorious statement of Romans 8:1, "There is therefore now no condemnation to them which are in Christ Jesus." Stated in just a little different form we read, "Therefore if any man be in Christ, he is a new creature: old things are passed away; behold, all things are become new" (2 Cor. 5:17).

There are many passages of Scripture in which this connection with Christ is represented as the foundation of our fellowship with him in spiritual and heavenly blessings. Ephesians 1:3-11 abounds with that thought: "who hath blessed us with all spiritual blessings in heavenly places *in Christ* . . . he hath chosen us *in him* . . . he hath made us accepted *in the beloved* . . . *in whom* we have redemption through his blood . . . he might gather together in one all things *in Christ* . . . *in whom* also we have obtained an inheritance." Here within the compass of a brief passage we are informed that to the prescient eye of God the whole church was embodied in Christ. *In Christ* men are chosen, accepted and loved by God. *In Christ* men receive redemption and heavenly inheritance. *In Christ* God gathers all things together in one. This union was typified in the old dispensation in the person of the high priest, who carried on his breast the twelve stones, on which were engraven the names of the twelve tribes of the children of Israel; so that, when he appeared before God, all the people appeared in him. Not only the old Israel but the new spiritual Israel are before God in Jesus Christ, their great High Priest. Through their federal head, Christ Jesus, they are delivered from condemnation and inherit the blessings of God.

Again and again the phrase, *in Christ,* is emphasized because the new community receives its inauguration, institution, position, life, unity, function through being incorporated into Christ. Outward organization has little emphasis in the N. T. because it pales into insignificance in comparison to being in Christ. The growth of the church does not come through human organization but through Christ, "in whom all the building fitly framed together groweth unto an holy temple in the Lord: in whom ye also are builded together for an habitation of God through the Spirit" (Eph. 2:21, 22). Carnal men are blinded to this high spiritual concept and want to deposit the life and glory of the church into a visible framework. The Spirit in the Scriptures guards jealously the spiritual conception of the church; the omission of a "centrally (human) controlled organization" is deliberate. The heavenly Jerusalem has displaced the earthly Jerusalem and is not in bondage to the traditions and control of men. "But ye are come unto mount Zion, and unto the city of the living God, the heavenly Jerusalem" (Heb. 12:22). While many would give this verse an eschatological interpretation, yet the author of Hebrews indicates entrance into the heavenly Jerusalem was a present experience of the Hebrew Christians.

LIFE IN CHRIST

The Church receives not only her origin and position but her continuing life in Christ. The Bible contains a wealth of this truth, "I am come that they might have life, and that they might have it more abundantly" (John 10:10); "Because I live, ye shall live also" (John 14:19); "I am the vine, ye are the branches. He that abideth in me, and I in him, the same

bringeth forth much fruit: for without me ye can do nothing"
(John 15:5); "I live," says Paul, "and yet not I, but Christ
liveth in me" (Gal. 2:20). These are but a few of many passages,
signifying that the life of the individual believer and the Church
depend on abiding in Christ.

External connection with the visible church does not suffice;
one must be internally connected with Christ himself. Those
who are members of the church catholic may be entirely destitute
of spiritual life except they be vitally united with Christ.
Emphasis on external organization tends to hide this truth and
some would give the impression that a more abundant life will
result from the establishment of a world-wide church. C. C.
Morrison definitely gives this impression:

> In a united church, each of us would experience something
> like a transfiguration of his spiritual life. In such a church,
> the soul of every member would be enlarged and ennobled.
> His Christian faith, liberated from its walled-in sectarian
> isolation, would be exalted. His ardent devotion would
> then be given, under Christ, to a church whose moral and
> spiritual dignity would command the respect in the local
> community, in the nation and the world which the Lord-
> ship of Christ deserves and which our sectarian churches
> cannot evoke. Every believer would be a participant in this
> majestic and holy brotherhood. The glory of its world-wide
> mission and the depths of its ecumenical fellowship would
> be registered in his own soul. As an ecumenical Christian,
> his membership in the whole church would be invested
> with a sense of high reality, of profound religious meaning
> and certain triumph. All this, let us repeat, would mean
> that the attainment of an ecumenical church would pro-
> duce a new kind of Christian (*The Unfinished Reforma-
> tion*, p. 98).

Seemingly the ecumenical church will produce what Scriptures
attribute to Christ. Not Christ but the church would effect a
transfiguration of the individual.

How foreign such exaltation of the visible church is to the
Scriptures. The more abundant life of the believers is derived
from Christ—through abiding in him. The Bible teaches that
life is obtained not by abiding *with* him, or *near* him, or *under*

him; but abiding *in* him. Abiding in Christ develops the spiritual senses: eyes to see the things prepared by God for those who love him; ears to hear what the Spirit says in the churches; a tongue to sing his praises; and a taste for spiritual things. All those exercises of holy thought, holy devotion, holy disposition, holy living, that constitute spiritual life, are prompted and sustained by the indwelling Christ. Faith, virtue, knowledge, temperance; patience, godliness, brotherly kindness, charity are possessed by the believer through the divine power of Christ (2 Pet. 1:3-8). Christ receives the preeminence in all things; the church humbly confesses, "He must increase, but I must decrease." Yet such is the love of God that the exaltation of Christ carries along the exaltation of the Church. The glory of the Church radiates from the glory of Christ.

UNITY IN CHRIST

The ground of unity among believers is their spiritual union with Christ. In submission of faith to him, appropriation of truth he revealed, receiving his Spirit, consists the essence of Christianity. Out of this springs the common consciousness that unites all true Christians in a holy fellowship, however separated by time, space, language, or denomination. Although separated by time the experience of being redeemed by the blood of Christ unites the twentieth century believer with the first century Paul and Peter who give witness to the same experience. The knowledge of being a new creature in Christ Jesus on the part of an American Christian gives kinship to the Australian believer though at opposite ends of the earth. African, Chinese, English, German, Italian disciples of Christ, all speak the same spiritual language though with different tongues. Being born from above gives sense of close affinity to believers of all denominations. Belonging to Christ rather than belonging to an organization establishes the bond of unity. The consciousness of being in Christ rather than membership in a world-wide church achieves the sense of unity.

Under the figure of the vine and branches another aspect of unity is portrayed. By virtue of abiding in the one vine the branches have an established relationship with each other and partake of the same nature. Christ creates a kinship by sustaining all those who abide in him. Of course, we have the concept of oneness as an actuality—the vinestock and branches make up one tree, Christ and his people are one; the leading thought, however, is the sameness and identity of life. As the sap of the vine enters into every branch, bringing forth identical fruit, so the life of Christ enters every believer, bringing forth Christian fruit. Christ moulds the wills of those who abide in him, bringing them into conformity with his own; he purifies the affections, giving them form and direction; he enlarges minds, filling them with the mysteries of the kingdom of heaven. Similarity of wills, identity of affections, like-mindedness, all draw people together into close unity. Hindrance to unity does not consist of the lack of one external organization to which people can cleave but to the absence of internal connection with Christ.

Could it be possible that absence of spiritual union in Christ has caused modern day stress on external union? Little compulsion was felt by first century Christians to establish an organization since spiritual bonds were so strong and evident. Consciousness of being in Christ made them keenly aware of fellowship, deeper than civic and family ties. A single external organization under a hierarchy would have added little or nothing to their sensitiveness of oneness in the Saviour; it actually would have been a hindrance. Today this vital, living experience with Christ seems missing in many of the historical denominations and formalism predominates. People hold to a form of godliness without experience of its power. Outward forms take on greater magnitude and importance to those destitute of spirituality. Where spiritual bonds are wanting, external bonds seem imperative and necessary. This observation does not mean to imply that all concerned with external unity are lacking in spirituality since motivation for a world-wide church may come from other factors. Nevertheless, the more people dwell in Christ the less they feel the importance of external bonds.

True ecumenity must labor to lead the membership of the church into real and living relationship to Christ. Winning ecclesiastical battles for amalgamation and merger means nothing in the sight of God if churches are not *in Christ*. As we have seen this is no empty phrase, denoting only nominal Christianity; it expresses a vital relationship to the federal Head and life flowing from the Head to the Body. Paul was little concerned about the plurality of churches but his anxiety was that they be in Christ. He uses that brief comprehensive phrase once and again in reference to little groups scattered here and there, "the churches of Judea which were in Christ Jesus," "the churches of God, which in Judea are in Christ Jesus" (Gal. 1:22; 1 Thess. 2:14). Paul also makes frequent reference to the "saints in Christ." This, then was the great central bond of union between members of the apostolic church. They were and felt themselves to be one in Christ Jesus. If this were the emphasis in the ecumenical movement, one would discover more enthusiasm among evangelicals.

Chapter VIII

ONE FAITH

One sharp point of division between ecumenists and evangelicals concerns the necessity of one faith as a major unifying force in Christendom. Some assert that wide diversity of beliefs does not militate against Christian unity or the establishment of a monolithic church. The ecumenical movement—especially in America—would not subscribe to the proposition of one faith as defined in Scripture. At the most there would be a hazy agreement in an undefined faith in Christ as God and Saviour. Even this brief formula must be open to various interpretations and full liberty must be given to all conceptions of Christ.

The ecumenical movement fights shy of sharply defining Christian faith for fear of its disturbing element. An undefined faith produces a paradise of peace and tranquility (though a heretic's paradise). It is interesting to note that the first contest that disturbed the peace of the early church was with heretics rather than schismatics. Heretics, as a rule, have no disposition to leave the organized church; their desire is to control and to leaven with false doctrine. The apostles did not labor to broaden the definition of faith so that all shades of belief could live comfortably within the church; they refused to accept peace at the cost of truth and courageously fought heresy by sharply and fully defining Christian faith. However, contending for the faith opposes the tenor of the twentieth century church wherein peace seems more precious than truth. This presents a grave danger for from a position that all modes of faith have equal standing within the church difficulty will not be experienced to arrive at the position that none are necessary. Faith, for which contention is denied, has little value in the sight of men and will soon perish. The flood gate opens wide for a hundred and one heresies to the triumph of infidelity.

FAITH DEFINED

Along with the declaration that there exists one body, one Spirit, one Lord, one baptism, one God, Paul declares the existence of one faith (Eph. 4:4-6). Commentators have been divided as to whether "faith" in the Ephesian passage refers to the subjective experience of the believer or to the objective content, denoting the doctrine of the Gospel. While we are convinced that the faith experience of the believer is indicated chiefly by the "one faith" yet that faith could never become a subjective reality without the content of the Christian message. Paul observes, "How then shall they call on him in whom they have not believed? and how shall they believe in him of whom they have not heard? And how shall they hear without a preacher?" (Rom. 10:14). Faith does not originate out of thin air but by means of the message delivered by God-sent preachers who proclaim the gospel of peace and bring glad tidings of good things. This gospel is one. Without objective faith that is one there can be no subjective faith that is one. Diverse gospels produce diverse faiths.

Objective faith consists of sound doctrine, such as is necessary to be known and believed for salvation. It consists of the way of salvation declared in the Gospel. Among passages where the content of faith receives emphasis are these, "a great company of believers were obedient to the faith" (Acts 6:7); "he which persecuted us in times past now preacheth the faith which once he destroyed" (Gal. 1:23); "in the latter times some shall depart from the faith" (I Tim. 4:1); "To Titus, mine own son after the common faith" (Titus 1:4); "contend for the faith which was once delivered unto the saints" (Jude 3). Faith has a definite content which the Church is urged to defend with all her might. The content of this faith is deposited in the Scriptures.

The specific purpose of the content of the Christian faith is to point to the person of Jesus Christ as the only one able to save the soul of sinful man. That is why the apostle Paul witnessed, "For I determined not to know any thing among you, save Jesus Christ, and him crucified" (I Cor. 2:2). The object of faith is not a creed, not a doctrine, not a mere propositional passage of Scripture, but the glorious person of Jesus Christ. The creeds, doctrines, Scriptures, all point to the Christ in whom one must believe to experience salvation. They point to the historic Christ who walked by the Sea of Galilee and who is now enthroned in heaven at the right hand of the Father. Creeds and confessions are not an end in themselves but are schoolmasters to lead to the historic and living Christ. The true believer confesses without shame, "Jesus Christ the same yesterday, and today and for ever" (Heb. 13:8).

The term faith (*pistis*) properly means trust and reliance on the personal Saviour for life and salvation (cf. Acts 16:31; Eph. 3:12; John 3:16; Acts 24:24). Man confesses that he is devoid of spiritual life and that he stands condemned before God as transgressor of his law; his burdened and guilty soul rests with assurance on Christ for forgiveness and newness of life. It has been stated that faith consists in knowledge, assent, and trust. Without knowledge one cannot apprehend the way of salvation; without assent there is no acceptance of that revealed; and without trust salvation is not attained. Faith must have knowledge of Christ; must have the assent of mind to believe the revelation concerning Christ; must have the concurrence of the will embracing the Christ revealed. This is more than assent to any other truth; it requires a supernatural effect produced by the Holy Spirit. The final effect is complete reliance upon and confidence in Jesus Christ as Saviour and Lord. This experience—this faith—is one in every true believer. Where faith signifies confidence in the one Saviour and Lord in the scriptural sense, subjective oneness is sustained by the unity of its object.

Faith in the person of Christ, and as defined in Scripture, is of the essence of Christianity. Only such faith justifies the sinner before God. The reformers rightly considered the doctrine of justification by faith as basic to the Christian religion and considered any denial or deviation of that truth as fatal to the existence of the church. Some would caricature the Reformers' position by implying that their faith was in a proposition, a doctrine. Such have not read the writings of the Reformers. Their proposition and doctrine was that only by faith in the blessed Saviour who died for sin could any sinner stand justified before the holy God. They insisted that confidence and reliance was to be in the person of Christ and not merely in a proposition or doctrine.

ESSENCE OF CHRISTIANITY

Sooner or later the ecumenical movement must wrestle with the problem of what constitutes the essence of Christianity. A movement that claims to be Christian cannot forever live in a haze of vague generalities or in a fog of double-talk and pious-sounding paradoxes. Without a clearly defined message an effective witness to the world is impossible. The Lord Jesus Christ commissioned the church to teach and preach the gospel. What is the content of this gospel—this good news—that the church must deliver to a world in darkness? The apostles knew the content and proclaimed it with great power. The early church conquered pagan Rome by preaching and living the gospel. The Reformers dispelled the darkness of ignorance and superstition with the identical message proclaimed by the apostles and the early church. The same gospel has the power to conquer the communism, secularism, paganism of the twentieth century. However, they cannot be overcome by an undefined statement that Jesus is God and Saviour. These movements have their gods and saviours. The uniqueness of Christ as God must be shown and explained. That Jesus is the only Saviour from sin, death, and hell must be asserted with clarity. A church without a clear notion of what is fundamental and vital to her witness will never overcome the world.

Not only an effective witness demands definition of faith but the very preservation of the church calls for the affirmation and the vindication of her vital message. Destroy the essence of Christianity and you destroy the church. Above all things the person of Christ constitutes the essence of the Christian religion. The controversies of the early centuries centered about the person of Christ. These controversies are deprecated and censured by some ecumenists who fear their recurrence in the twentieth century. The early church fathers realized that they were fighting for the essence of Christianity and the life of the church and refused to shirk unpleasant responsibility. The results of their labors and heartaches unified the church in regard to the person of Christ for many centuries. Dodging the issue of the person of Christ, both in respect to his Godhood and manhood, for the sake of a universal inclusiveness, may well destroy the church.

More than the deity and manhood of Christ is bound up in the vital message and preservation of the church. Among important teachings revealed in Scripture as vital to Christian faith are: the incarnation, sinless life and obedience of the Son of man, vicarious atonement, bodily resurrection, the ascension, justification by faith, the sovereignty of God, and the person and work of the Holy Spirit. To leave the church of Christ without a distinctive doctrinal basis with the purpose of an inclusive policy would be to destroy the church in order to extend it. Without a vital and true faith the church retains only a name—a form of godliness; in the eyes of God he exists only as a synagogue of Satan. One cannot categorize even one of the fundamental doctrines of Scripture as unimportant and unessential to the life of the church. The system of doctrine contained in the Bible is an organism—destroy one vital part and terrible sickness and weakness will result.

Moreover, the dream of a great organization—without a clear defined faith—is a violation of the responsibility that God has placed upon the church to be "the pillar and ground of the truth" (I Tim. 3:15). The church is here represented as holding up and sustaining truth, doing the same for truth as foundations and pillars do for buildings. There can be no edifice of any compelling size and beauty without a foundation and support of pillars. This does not indicate that the church discovered truth by herself or established truth. The Lord Jesus Christ is the Prophet of the church and has revealed truth to her. "God, who at sundry times and in divers manners spake in time past unto the fathers by the prophets, hath in these last days spoken unto us by his Son" (Heb. 1:1, 2). The oracles have been committed to the church; she has not created them. By truth and the proclamation of it the church grows and expands. By truth she goes forth conquering and to conquer. For the church to ignore truth, to neglect truth, to forsake truth for the sake of an inclusive policy is suicide and shirking her duty to God and man.

Christ felt that the unity of faith was so essential to the life and well-being of the church that he endowed the ministry with the gift of the Holy Spirit in order that the church might come into the unity of faith. The net result would be that "we henceforth be no more children, tossed to and fro, and carried about with every wind of doctrine" (Eph. 4:11-14). The unity of faith is a protection against the winds of false doctrine. The very fact that Paul speaks of the unity of faith in the context of protection against the winds of false doctrine, indicates strongly the importance he attaches to true doctrine. His concern shows up in every epistle of which he is the author. In the first chapter of Galatians he marvels that some turned so soon to another gospel and warns of the curse of God upon those who turn aside from teaching revealed truth. Of the seven churches mentioned in Revelation 2 and 3 only two are exempted from censure of having departed from the purity and unity of faith. In the light of biblical emphasis on truth and unity of faith as essential to Christianity, how can any Christian movement disregard and shun the responsibility of giving permanent and attractive visibility to truth? How can organizational visibility be considered more important and vital than visibility of united truth? When the essence of Christianity is obscured the church becomes weak and ineffective as history demonstrates. Unity of faith should take on priority over any other question confronting the church and surely priority over the question of organization.

ESSENTIAL TO UNITY

Not only is the essence of Christianity at stake by the preservation of one true faith but unity itself is at stake. Genuine and permanent unity simply cannot exist without the presence of agreement on essential teachings of Christianity. Stifling controversy and minimizing differences may hasten the organization of a world-wide church—but will the end result be a *Christian* church? Some ecumenists hasten to assure that after organizational unity, theological unity will surely follow. They assert as long as doctrinal unity is kept to the fore, organizational unity will be delayed. Therefore they work diligently to keep doctrine in the background and minimize its importance to unity. However, if organizational unity be achieved one can well imagine that there will be strong argument to hush controversy lest the organization be endangered. Within many denominations differences of belief exist that cause constant friction and debate. Mixture of liberals and evangelicals has not led to harmony and settlement of theological differences. A world-wide church has no peculiar magic that would dispell disagreement of doctrine and would set up a situation in which only ecclesiastical pressure could avoid separation and schism. Unity of faith should be obtained first. History has shown that the strongest cohesive is agreement in doctrine and permanent unity cannot be gained without it.

So long as the various Christian denominations retain the fundamental doctrines of Christianity, the essential unity of the church is manifested even though it may be obscured. The early church fathers, in their conflict with heresy, insisted chiefly on the historical continuity of doctrine in the churches founded by the apostles. The unity of apostolic doctrine was the great weapon against heretical sects and has in fact preserved the church during the course of the centuries. Recent stress has been laid on the continuity of the church in the apostolic succession of office, but of what avail is that where there is no apostolic succession of teaching? Can the hierarchy bind more closely than the apostolic faith in the living Lord as Saviour and redeemer?

Those who would supplant apostolic teaching with the liberal teachings of the twentieth century are actually cutting the bond of unity with former generations of believers. The glory of the Christian church has been the unity of faith throughout the centuries; her shame has been deviations from revealed truth and neglect of Scriptures as the source of faith and life. History attests that the strongest periods of the church were contemporary with a high view of Scripture and fidelity to revealed truth. Surely the teachings of Scripture form a continuity of faith from the first century to the present. Modern theology, in its opposition to apostolic doctrine and authority of Scripture, has caused a serious cleavage in the continuity of Christian faith. Often evangelicals are reproached by liberals as trouble makers in Israel. But Elijah's reply to Ahab holds good, "I have not troubled Israel; but thou, and thy father's house, in that ye have forsaken the commandments of the Lord." Departure from historic Christian faith destroys the unity of faith.

DIVERSITIES OF BELIEFS

In spite of biblical emphasis on unity of faith as vital to Christianity, the accepted dogma of the ecumenical movement is that one may have diversity of beliefs without sin and scandal but that diversity of organizations is evil and disgraceful. The position of the Scriptures seems to be reversed. Bishop Newbigin writes, "The true character of this union of believers with one another in Christ is disastrously distorted when it is conceived of essentially in terms of doctrinal agreement. The effect of such distortion is to break the Christian fellowship up into rival parties, each based upon some one-sided doctrinal formulation, and eventually into completely separated bodies" (*The Household of God,* pp. 52, 53). C. C. Morrison throughout his book develops the theme that doctrinal agreement is unimportant and writes, "What in a united church, shall we do with our differences? There can be only one answer. They must be welcomed and embraced as essential to the fulfillment of the Christian life. Our diversities are not a spiritual liability, but a spiritual asset, of the Christian life. . . . It will be a church characterized by diversity, not by uniformity, for the Spirit is not manifested in uniformity, but in diversity. . . . Our present thesis is that the inmost structure of the united church can have no formal standards of loyalty save the authority inherent in the Lordship of Christ, and that the entire subject matter of the sectarian standards must be given its place in the freedom of its fellowship" (*The Unfinished Reformation,* pp. 82, 129, 199).

One of the amazing dogmas of ecumenity maintains that the spirit manifests himself not in uniformity but in diversity of beliefs. This shows to what depth some have entered into the meaning of the diverse gifts, *charismata,* received from the Spirit as recorded in I Corinthians 12. There is absolutely no justification in maintaining that the diversities mentioned in that chapter are concerned with diversities of beliefs! The Scriptures emphasize unity of faith and not diversity of faith. The Spirit of truth would not reveal to one man that Jesus is God; to another that he became God; to another that he is a mere symbol. Why make the Spirit the author of confusion and contradictions? There is much more justification in interpreting the Spirit's diversities mentioned in I Corinthians, to be in the realm of administration than in theology as it speaks of the diversities of administrations, helps and governments. Yet ecumenists are horrified at the thought that the Holy Spirit may not be manifested in uniformity of administration and government, but in diversity. They fail to see their strange inconsistency.

Biblical theology has been a neglected science but is again coming to the fore. A few are beginning to discern an amazing unity in the Scripture. If scholars will subject themselves with proper meekness to the authority of Scripture, they will discover a unity in the written Word that has been obscured by the subjective reasoning and presuppositions of many higher critics. The depravity of man, salvation through the Messiah, covenant of grace, expiatory sacrifice, vicarious atonement, judgment, kingdom, church, all are concepts running throughout the written revelation. Naturally there is such a thing as progressive revelation within the Word. Biblical theology, if unhampered by doubt in the veracity of the written records, will reveal that the Holy Spirit is the author of unity of faith and not diversity of beliefs.

TOWARDS UNITY OF FAITH

The church has been led by the Holy Spirit into a rich doctrinal experience of the fundamental truths of Scripture. This experience (that so many condemn as divisive) actually is a forward step into the direction of unity of faith. So often it is expressed that our agreements are greater in number and of more vital importance than our differences. Then straightway these agreements are forgotten, neglected, ignored, and forsaken! If the ecumenical movement were to build upon the agreements in the creeds of historic denominations then the movement would be more impressive and hopeful. A study of Episcopal, Presbyterian,

Lutheran, Baptist, Methodist creeds would show a wonderful uniformity and agreement on such doctrines as the infallibility of Scripture, Trinity, deity of Christ, vicarious atonement, lost estate of man, reality of heaven and hell, and many more. But would the ecumenical movement accept these agreements? Or does it speak of agreements of doctrine for rhetorical effect only?

Professor Peter Brunner, Professor of Systematic Theology at the University of Heidelberg, Germany, stated that the member churches of the World Council put up with convictions among their pastors, professors and church leaders which the fathers of these churches have repudiated as heretical. He writes, "It would be to misunderstand our situation today, were we to make a kind of virtue out of it, saying, 'Since we can no longer determine the boundary line between apostolic and heretical, we must push the question concerning agreement on the hearing and proclaiming of the content of the apostolic message into the background, and take instead the preponderant organizational road to solve the problem of church fellowship. The lines of division which our fathers saw have become largely historical ballast, especially for the mission churches. The progress of the history of ideas and theology has freed us from this ballast. What hinders us from viewing this question of agreement on the apostolic Word completely anew? What would hinder us from by-passing all questions of substantial doctrinal content—except for a somewhat broadened theological 'basis' of the World Council of Churches—and perhaps seek instead an agreement on practical deeds through which the apostolicity of the involved churches could be demonstrated?" Then he adds significantly, "Those who think in this fashion have misunderstood the need of our churches today. Whoever thinks this way has taken a decisive step toward the dissolution of the church. The extent to which the living apostolic Word becomes silent in separating the truth of God from the error of man is the extent to which the true nature of the church is placed in question" (*The Unity of the Church*, A Symposium, pp. 20, 21).

The above statements of Professor Brunner reveal realistic thinking on the problem of unity. The Confessions of the churches have dealt with error and have stated the position of the church on vital doctrines. These Confessions need not remain static and are always to be judged by Scripture. If restatements have to be made in light of modern errors the church must face up to the task. But to neglect the creeds is a step backward. The agreements must be consolidated and the movement for visibility of unity must proceed from what has been accomplished in the past.

Unity of faith cannot be accomplished in a generation—especially in a generation that is scripturally illiterate. This may take the course of centuries. This generation, however, must rid itself of the idea that the only heresy is a firm and consistent faith, based on Scripture. It must eschew the popular "ecumenical" idea that diversity of beliefs is to be welcome and considered a healthy condition within the church. It must escape the complex that the only "unity of faith" that can be achieved is that there is no unity of faith possible. *One faith* exists in the revealed Word and the Lord has given the ministry to the church "Till we all come in the unity of the faith."

Chapter IX

THE HOLY CATHOLIC CHURCH

I believe in the Holy Catholic Church has resounded through the course of centuries as an expression of faith in the existence, unity and perpetuity of the Christian Church. The statement reveals that the Church is not a matter of sight, but of faith. If the essence of the Church were her visibility then there is no need of faith to realize her existence. The statement manifests that the Church is one. If one organization were essential to unity then faith in the essential oneness of the church would be a delusion. Faith, however, clings to the revelation that the Church exists as one. Also the statement expresses faith that the church is universal. Faith looks beyond the boundary of denominations and beyond the confines of the contemporary generation. For the declaration of perpetuity and continuity faith looks at revelation rather than a hierarchy. The Word reveals and faith declares the existence, the unity, and the perpetuity of the Church.

The Church precedes history. The Church existed within the counsel of the Godhead before the creation of the earth. The Scripture states, "According as he hath chosen us in him before the foundation of the world, that we should be holy and without blame before him in love: having predestinated us unto the adoption of children by Jesus Christ to himself, according to the good pleasure of his will, to the praise of the glory of his grace, wherein he hath made us accepted in the beloved" (Eph. 1:4-6).

Before the foundation of the world the Church was formed in the mind of God. The Church existed "in the beloved" and "before the foundation of the world." The same truth is expressed in 2 Timothy 1:9, "Who hath saved us, and called us with an holy calling, not according to our works, but according to his own purpose and grace, which was given us in Christ Jesus before the world began." The purpose of God and his grace assures the existence, the unity, and perpetuity of the Church. Neither of these things depends on the will of man or on one visible organization—not even a hierarchy. Unity has its basis in the purpose and action of God.

ONE HOLY CATHOLIC CHURCH

Not only within the eternal counsels of God but in history there exists but one church—The Holy Catholic Church. The concept of one church appears in various figures of speech used to denote the people of God. The figure of *body* finds frequent reference in Scripture. After showing the diversities of gifts endowed by the Spirit, the apostle Paul informed the Corinthians that the body is one, "For as the body is one, and hath many members, and all the members of that one body, being many, are one body: so also is Christ" (1 Cor. 12:12). That there might be no misunderstanding of the aggregate membership forming the body of Christ, Paul adds in verse 27 of the same chapter, "Now ye are the body of Christ, and members in particular." The church in Corinth was not in organizational union with the church at Jerusalem or Rome yet she could be spoken of as the body of Christ. Christ possesses one body that cannot be dismembered.

Two figures of speech appear in Revelation 21 to describe the church. "And I John saw the holy city, new Jerusalem, coming down from God out of heaven, prepared as a bride adorned for her husband. . . . Come hither, I will shew thee the bride, the Lamb's wife. And he carried me away in the spirit to a great and high mountain, and shewed me that great city, the holy Jerusalem, descending out of heaven from God." (vss. 2, 9, 10). Pluralities of brides or cities do not exist in the sight of the Head of the Church. There is but one Bride and one Holy City. *Temple* is another figure of speech to describe the children of God.

Paul wrote to Gentile Christians in Ephesus of the unity that has come about through the blood of Christ. Gentiles who had no part or place in the Temple now become a part of the Household of God. Paul adds in regard to the unity in Christ, "In whom all the building fitly framed together groweth unto an holy temple in the Lord: in whom ye also are builded together for an habitation of God through the Spirit" (Eph. 2:21, 22). The Temple is one.

After Peter confessed that Jesus was the Messiah, the Son of the living God, the Lord stated, "And I say also unto thee, that thou art Peter and upon this rock I will build my church; and the gates of hell shall not prevail against it" (Matt. 16:18). Jesus did not say, "I will build my churches," but, "I will build my church." This was in fulfillment of Zechariah 6:12, "Thus speaketh the Lord of hosts, saying, Behold the man whose name is the BRANCH; and he shall grow up out of his place, and he shall build the temple of the Lord." Whether in the New Testament or the Old the concept of the Church is one.

To those who accept the authority of Scripture, the unity of the church is never a problem. Unity is God-given and established by the Son of God. Unity is a creation of God and not of man. The creative act of God is a presupposition and the foundation of the statement of the Apostles' Creed, "I believe in *the* Holy Catholic Church." The act of God prevents the Holy Catholic Church of ever being fragmented or splintered.

The important responsibility remains of expressing and manifesting the God-established oneness of the Church. Evangelicals are often at fault by smugly resting on the scriptural teaching of oneness and feeling no responsibility of giving visibility to that oneness. While the ecumenical movement for the great part unduly and mistakenly magnifies organizational unity as the principal goal to be achieved, yet it must be commended for its zeal to give visibility to unity. Unfortunately, ecumenism has failed to grasp the fundamental spiritual unity created by God and has been led to emphasize a minor bond of union to the detriment of major bonds. Evangelicals, however, have failed to realize that the Word admonishes believers to "come in the unity of the faith, and of the knowledge of the Son of God, unto a perfect man, unto the measure of the stature of the ful-

ness of Christ" (Eph. 4:13). The evangelical church comes far
short of measuring up to the stature of the fulness of Christ
and cannot rest until she reaches that goal. The knowledge of
the ideal should give evangelicals the proper incentive, direction,
and perspective.

Naturally the delicate and controversial question arises as to
which particular church or denomination on earth comes nearest
to portraying the Holy Catholic Church. While judgment belongs
to the Head of the Church, nevertheless some estimate may be
determined by a comparison with the marks or characteristics
of the Holy Catholic Church revealed in Scripture. Conclusions
can be drawn by those who will subject themselves to the judgment of Scripture.

HEADSHIP OF CHRIST

One dominant mark of the Holy Catholic Church revealed in
Scripture is the Headship of Christ. "And he is the head of the
body, the church" (Col. 1:18). "And hath put all things under
his feet and gave him to be the head over all things to the church,
which is his body, the fulness of him that filleth all in all"
(Eph. 1:22, 23). "For we are members of his body, of his flesh,
and of his bones" (Eph. 5:30). "But Christ as a son over his
own house; whose house are we" (Heb. 3:6). This Headship
of Jesus also appears in such statements as, "All power is given
unto me in heaven and earth" (Matt. 28:18); and "Therefore
let all the house of Israel know assuredly, that God hath made
that same Jesus, whom ye have crucified, both Lord and Christ"
(Acts 2:36).

Christ is head of the church as a king over loyal subjects. He
is lawgiver and protector. The relationship between husband
and wife is used by Scripture to define the affinity between
Christ and the Church. Christ is the head of the wife, the
Church. And even a closer relationship is expressed in that
Jesus is termed the head of the body. Without the head the
body cannot exist and thus the church is completely dependent
upon Christ. Absence of union with the Head, lack of dependence upon him, separation from him—all indicate that one is
outside of the Holy Catholic Church. Complete dependence
upon Christ comes out clearly in these two passages, "From

whom the whole body fitly joined together and compacted by that which every joint supplieth, according to the effectual working in the measure of every part, maketh increase of the body unto the edifying of itself in love" (Eph. 4:16); "And not holding the Head, from which the body by joints and bands having nourishment ministered and knit together increaseth with the increase of God" (Col. 2:19). Life, unity, growth of the body comes from the Head. If the head be dissevered the body dies.

All within the ecumenical movement seem willing to be under Christ and make much of his Lordship. But such subjection does not mean the same to all. Some, for instance, deny the teachings and commandments of Christ revealed in the Gospels. Jesus in the Great Commission urged the apostles to make disciples of all nations, baptizing them in the name of the Trinity, "teaching them to observe all things whatsoever I have commanded you." Some would pick and choose from the recorded teachings and commandments of Christ; they object to teaching all things commanded by the Lord. Of what avail then is it to cry Lord, Lord, and refuse to carry out his commission? If the trustworthiness of the Gospels as recording the teachings of Christ be denied then one must give up all pretense to the possession of a revealed religion. Then the term "Lord" is used only to enforce the subjective and fallible wisdom of men. The headship of Christ becomes a hollow mockery. However, such churches that subject themselves to the teachings of Christ and proclaim that which he has revealed, indicate a true mark of the Holy Catholic Church. They truly acknowledge the headship of Christ.

ADMINISTRATION OF SACRAMENTS

Ever since the Reformation Protestant churches have insisted that the proper administration of the sacraments constitutes one of the true marks of the Holy Catholic Church. This has reference both to the number and nature of the sacraments. The word *sacrament* is not found in Scripture but finds its meaning in ecclesiastical usage. In a general way sacrament may be defined as a holy ordinance instituted by Christ, in which by outward sensible signs inward spiritual graces are represented and benefits of the covenant of grace are conveyed to the believing soul. Only such ordinances are considered sacraments that have been instituted by Christ. This rules out five sacraments of the Roman Catholic Church—confirmation, penance, extreme unction, orders, and marriage. The two sacraments instituted by the Lord Jesus Christ are baptism, and the Lord's Supper.

While sacraments actually are means of grace to worthy recipients, exception is taken to the Roman teaching that the sacraments derive a divine virtue from the action of the priest in pronouncing certain words. It is supposed necessary that the priest has the intention of giving the elements that divine virtue, otherwise they remain in their original state. The Protestant position maintains that the efficacy of the sacrament resides in the sovereign and personal agency of the Holy Spirit who uses them as a means of grace to the true believer. The Roman Catholic is only required to be free from mortal sins and need not have a sanctified life or possess faith. In opposition to the unscriptural practices of the Roman Catholic Church, Protestants have insisted that a proper mark of the true church is the right administration of the sacraments.

Next to the preaching of the true gospel, the sacraments form a distinctive and visible bond of unity within the Christian church. Entrance into the church of Christ is signified by the rite of baptism. The Lord's Supper signifies that "we being many are one bread, and one body: for we are all partakers of that one bread" (1 Cor. 10:17). Baptism was designed to indicate reception into the Body of Christ and should establish a firm principle of brotherly love and oneness of spirit between the baptized membership. The Lord's Supper was designed to show that believers are one by being partakers of the one Bread, Christ Jesus. Contrary to their purpose the observance of the sacraments has led to sharp divisions and manifests cleavages within the visible church.

Ecumenists have discovered that baptism forms one of the major obstacles to the establishment of corporate union. A large segment of the visible church believes sincerely that immersion-baptism of believers is commanded by the Head of the church; another large segment believes that infants of believers cannot be excluded from the church as the Lord does not exclude them from the Kingdom. As long as they hold to the Lordship of Christ, neither can conscientiously give up their convictions. The gentle suggestion has been made that differences of interpretation and practice can be tolerated within the "freedom" of a united church. Winfred E. Garrison writes, "It would be fatally divisive to insist upon the universal adoption of the 'primitive practice' of the immersion of penitent believers as the only baptism (though I think it is), because not all Christians agree that this was always the primitive practice or that, if it was, Christ's intention was that this should be a permanent law for the church" (*The Quest and Character of a United Church,* p. 225). Some hope that the acceptance of modern scholarship will loosen the authority of Scripture and cause this matter to be settled by expediency. Many, however, feel strongly that obedience to the Lord speaking in Scripture is of greater importance than subordinating their convictions to serve the purpose of establishing an inclusive church.

The observance of the Lord's Supper has also focused attention on the cleavage in the visible church. Meetings of the World Council of Churches dramatized this cleavage by the necessity of holding four differing services of Holy Communion. Anglicans, Eastern Orthodox, Lutherans, and others could not gather about the common Lord's Table. This has been particularly painful to ecumenists who are trying to use the sacrament of the Lord's Supper as a visible emblem of unity.

To the keen observer these differences of interpretation and practices point to the need of theological agreement. The differences are rooted in theological convictions. The solution that ignores these differences or minimizes the importance of them can only be superficial. The church received the sacraments through revelation and must turn to the revelation for solution. To find proper interpretation may involve controversy but the climate of controversy need not be bitter. Denominational positions must be justified by Scripture. While the twentieth century is not marked by biblical scholarship in the realm of theology, it is marked by a climate in which differences may be discussed without bitter heat. Since most churches are agreed that the proper administration of the sacraments form a true mark of the

Holy Catholic Church, they should be willing to search diligently the revelation that God has given.

APOSTOLIC

Throughout the course of history from the very day of Pentecost, all churches have endeavored to prove that their teachings and practices were apostolic. Some denominations have, in addition, sought to prove apostolic succession in office. The first half of the twentieth century has witnessed a real effort to separate the church from apostolic authority in doctrine and to reduce this office to an undefined and hazy "witness." However, recent resurgence of Confessionialism has revived interest in judging the faithfulness of the church's witness by the apostolic Word. Strong feelings persist that the mark of a true church is the proclamation of apostolic doctrine. This conviction finds root in New Testament teachings.

Our Lord stated to the Apostle Peter, "And I say also unto thee, that thou art Peter, and upon this rock I will build my church" (Matt. 16:18). Protestant commentators have gone to great length to explain that our Lord did not indicate that he was building his church upon Peter—not on exegetical grounds, but because of Roman Catholic presumptions and wrong deductions. Our Lord, for instance, says nothing about apostolic succession or that the Bishop of Rome would receive the office of Peter. Nor can it be assumed that Peter alone was the rock upon which the church would be built. Several passages of Scripture indicate that the other apostles were included: "And are built upon the foundation of the apostles and prophets, Jesus Christ himself being the chief corner stone" (Eph. 2:20); "and the wall of the city had twelve foundations, and in them the names of the twelve apostles of the Lamb" (Rev. 21:14). Both of these passages clearly indicate that the church is built not on one apostle but on all.

No doubt our Lord constituted Peter and the other Apostles as a foundation to the church in their prophetic or teaching office. When Peter made his remarkable confession that Jesus was the Christ, the Son of the living God, Jesus declared that this confession was a revelation from God. As a recipient and witness of true revelation Peter was a rock upon which the church would be built. Not only Peter, but also the other Apostles received this authority for passing on revelation. The early believers "continued stedfastly in the apostles' doctrine" (Acts 2:42). Jesus had promised the Apostles, "But the Comforter, which is the Holy Ghost, whom the Father will send in my name, he shall teach you all things, and bring all things to your remembrance, whatsoever I have said unto you" (John 14:26); and "But when the Comforter is come, whom I will send unto you from the Father, even the Spirit of truth, which proceedeth from the Father, he shall testify of me; and ye also shall bear witness, because ye have been with me from the beginning" (John 15:26, 27). Jesus promised to send the Holy Spirit to guide the apostles into all truth so that they could give infallible witness to his teachings. The prophetic office, for which Jesus trained the Apostles and for which he promised the Holy Spirit, is the foundation of the church. Only by accepting apostolic teachings can she claim to be the recipient of a revealed religion.

There is an element in the ecumenical movement who desire to make the mark of apostolicity depend solely on a succession of office mediated by the laying on of hands. Anglicans show no readiness to accept any form of church unity that does not secure "The visible continuity of the church in the historic succession of the episcopate." Because of this intransigent attitude some are willing to yield so that the ecumenical movement will not be wrecked. Professor John Knox writes frankly, "I simply cannot conceive of the union of Christendom except on the ground of a polity which . . . involves the full acceptance of the historic episcopate"; "I see no hope of a united church without the universal acceptance of episcopacy" (The Early Church, pp. 142, 143). The insistence on the mark of apostolicity consisting in the succession by episcopal ordination reminds one of the Pharisees' confidence that they were the children of God through physical descent from Abraham. To the cry, "Abraham is our father," Jesus replied, "If ye are Abraham's children, ye would do the works of Abraham." Physical descent —external historic continuity—means nothing in the sight of God. To paraphrase a statement of John the Baptist, "Think not to say, we have Bishops for our ordination; for I say unto you, that God is able of these nonconformists to raise up an ordained ministry." Bishops have not been lacking who have been devoid of spirituality and morality. How can the laying on of their impure hands give validity to ordination? The proclamation of apostolic doctrine gives evidence of historical continuity. The Spirit provides a continuous ministry and ordination is the recognition by the church of the Spirit's work in calling and equipping a man for holy office. Historical succession comes from above.

The mark of apostolicity is seen in the church that confesses with the apostle Peter, "Thou art the Christ, the Son of the living God," that cries out with the apostle Thomas, "My Lord and my God"; that testifies with the apostle Paul, "For I determined not to know any thing among you, save Jesus Christ, and him crucified"; that witnesses with the apostle John, "And if any man sin, we have an advocate with the Father, Jesus Christ the righteous: and him the propitiation for our sins: and not for ours only, but also for the sins of the whole world." To paraphrase the utterance of Jesus, "If ye were the apostles' children, ye would do the work of the apostles."

HOLY

An important characteristic of the Christian church and one that should distinctly mark it off from the rest of the world is holiness. Two words in the Bible bring out the significance of holiness—the Hebrew *kadosh* and the Greek *hagios*. The primary meaning of *kadosh* is "to be set apart by God as his very own." It conveys the idea of divine ownership. *Kadosh* as a noun is translated *saint* and as an adjective, *holy*. We read in the Old Testament of the *holy* temple, a building set apart for God's house; of the *holy* city, set apart for God's people as also the country of Palestine, a *holy* land; and of the *holy* nation, separated from the rest of the world to be God's very own. The root idea of saint or holy is that which has been separated from the world and set apart for God. When God claims a man he is designated a saint; when God claims a building or city it is designated holy. The New Testament Greek word, *hagios*, conveys the same idea. Paul, in his Epistle to the Romans, writes, "To all that be in Rome, beloved of God, called to be saints."

Paul addresses the Christians in Ephesus as saints. A saint is one that has been called out of the evil world and set apart to the service of God.

More is involved, of course, than being set apart for God: holiness of character should follow the call of God. Peter writes, "But as he which hath called you is holy, so be ye holy in all manner of conversation" (1 Pet. 1:15). And Paul urges, "But fornication, and all uncleanness, or covetousness, let it not be once named among you, as becometh saints" (Eph. 5:3); and "For God hath not called us unto uncleanness, but unto holiness" (1 Thess. 4:7). Throughout the Gospels and Epistles there is an urgent call to righteous and holy living. Both the writers of the Old Testament and New stress the importance of conforming to the commandments of God and his Christ.

Without holiness the church can never expect to achieve unity upon earth. James asks pointedly, "From whence come wars and fightings among you? come they not hence, even of your lusts that war in your members?" (James 4:1). Undoubtedly some divisions within the visible church have been caused by absence of holiness and presence of evil lusts. Pride of intellect, ambition, dictatorial spirit, obstinancy and envy have caused schisms that cannot be vindicated. Unjustified division finds root in the evil lust of the human heart. The unsanctified human heart remains a formidable obstacle in the path of true unity. The holy church will be a united church. Seek first a holy church and unity will be added to her. The more the church conforms to the holiness of God the sooner she will manifest true unity.

One serious problem remains in light of the poverty of holiness evident in the life of the church. How can one express with sincerity and truth, "I believe in the *Holy* Catholic Church?" This cannot be limited to the Church at rest in heaven or the eschatological Church after the termination of history. The Apostles' Creed has reference to the church upon earth as well. Yet the militant church reveals divisions, imperfections and weaknesses. She comes far short of being holy as God is holy. Luther's problem was similar in that he despaired of an unrighteous man being received by the righteous God until he discovered the blessed truth that the righteousness of Christ was imputed to the believer through faith. He experienced the truth of Philippians 3:9, "And be found in him, not having mine own righteousness, which is of the law, but that which is through the faith of Christ, the righteousness which is of God by faith." The church upon earth does not achieve holiness through the law but is clothed in the garment of Christ's holiness by faith. The church is hid in Christ by faith. The holiness of Christ distinguishes the true church—a holiness seen only with eyes of faith. Faith can state in sincerity and truth, "I believe in the *Holy* Catholic Church."

DISCIPLINE

The visible church upon earth cannot hope to achieve any measure of holiness in the life of her membership without the exercise of discipline. It is for the sake of holiness that Protestant Confessions generally make discipline one of the essential marks of the church. If the Christian community tolerates immorality and heresy, it would soon lose any distinctiveness and uniqueness. It would cease to be a Christian society as holiness and truth separate and distinguish the church from any other society. To retain within the church those who are guilty of flagrant sin and who hold doctrines subversive to the very basis of Christian faith is an indulgence and tolerance of which neither Christ nor the apostles were culpable. Tolerance of evil in any form helps neither the guilty, the church nor society. Bishop Newbigin well states, "The Church in a non-Christian cultural environment has to take seriously the business of discipline. That is a commonplace in the experience of every one of the younger Churches. It is necessary because, in the first place, the removal of the convert from the sphere of the traditional discipline of caste, community, or tribe, puts upon the Church the responsibility for seeing to it that this is replaced by a new kind of social discipline; and secondly, because without this the Church's witness to the non-Christian world becomes hopelessly compromised" (*The Household of God*, p. 7).

Christ provided for discipline by giving the keys of the kingdom of heaven to Peter so that whatsoever was bound on earth would be bound in heaven and whatsoever was loosed on earth would be loosed in heaven, Matthew 16:19. In connection with instruction on the procedure to discipline that same power was given to the church, Matthew 18:15-18. Our Lord reproved the Asiatic churches because they neglected the exercise of discipline, Revelation 2:14, 15, 20. No doubt because they tolerated immorality and false doctrine, the churches disappeared from the scene of history. That the apostles practiced and counselled discipline can be seen throughout the epistles (Cor. 5:3-5; I Tim. 1:19, 20; II Thess. 3:6).

The evangelical (who is not without sin) is apprehensive that the ecumenical movement by an indiscriminate inclusiveness and lack of proper exercise of discipline is bartering the holiness of the church for a show of numbers. Fear is often expressed that exclusiveness and discipline will drive people away from the church. History reveals that the most effective influence of the church is that of holiness. Take the incidence in Acts 5 that shocks some who have little understanding of holiness. Because of lying to God, Ananias and Sapphira dropped dead. This act of discipline caused great fear to come upon the church and "believers were the more added to the Lord, multitudes both of men and women." That which guards the holiness and truth of the church enhances its public influence and multiplies its converts. The world beholds other societies exercising discipline over its membership while the church, checked by cowardice or false tolerance, fails to remove even the most flagrant violators of her laws. No wonder the world scorns the church. Of course, discipline should be in love and with arms ever open for the penitent. But unless discipline is exercised the reputation of the church suffers and holiness vanishes.

CATHOLIC CHURCH

"The catholic or universal Church, which is invisible, consists of the whole number of the elect that have been, are, or shall be, gathered into one under Christ the head thereof; and is the spouse, the body, the fulness of Him that filleth all in all"—so states the Westminster Confession of Faith. A glorious description of the Catholic Church is given by the apostle John in these words, "After these things I saw, and behold, a great multitude, which no man could number, out of every nation and of all tribes and peoples and tongues, standing before the throne and before the Lamb." The term "catholic" includes all whom God has given to Christ. Protestants would make a strategic error to yield that term to the Roman Catholic Church which by the use of the "Roman" contradicts the root meaning of *catholic*.

The term ecumenical must not be confused or substituted for the well-defined ecclesiastical use of the word *catholic*. Regardless of what import it may have to different individuals or groups the root meaning of ecumenical is "world-wide" and is limited to this earth. We may not confine the existence of the Church within such narrow limits. The Holy Catholic Church is co-extensive with the redeemed of Christ.

Evangelicals have not always held to the unity of the Church as existing between the old and new dispensations. However, the Church is one by the very fact that under both dispensations men have been justified by virtue of the blood of Christ. He is the Lamb slain from the foundation of the world. Habakkuk, the prophet, assured the Jewish Church "the just shall live by his faith." Paul wrote to the Galatians that God preached the gospel to Abraham and added, "And if ye be Christ's, then are ye Abraham's seed, and heirs according to the promise" (Gal. 3:29). Jesus said, "Your father Abraham rejoiced to see my day: and he saw it, and was glad" (John 8:56). Faith in God led the Israelites of old to have firm hope in Christ, so in the desert they are said to have drunk of the "spiritual Rock that followed them: and that Rock was Christ" (1 Cor. 10:4). There is but one Church, one Temple, one holy Jerusalem, one Olive Tree, one Bride, one Household of God in which "there is neither Jew nor Greek, there is neither bond nor free, there is neither male nor female: for ye are all one in Christ Jesus" (Gal. 3:28). There is but one Holy Catholic Church.

The term *church* is derived from the Greek *kuriakon*, literally, *the Lord's House*. The corresponding term is *ekklesia* to which the New Testament gives the content of the assembly of the called. Sometimes the term *ekklesia* refers to a local church assembly and sometimes to the one true Church which does not possess a visible head or a common visible government. In the latter sense the Church is referred to as the Body and Bride of Christ and "the general assembly and church of the first born, which are written in heaven" (Heb. 12:23). It is in this sense that the Apostles' Creed uses the term "Holy Catholic Church."

I BELIEVE

More than the mere expression of the statement of the Apostles' Creed is required of the believer. The visible church exists with many denominational distinctions that approach in greater or lesser degree the ideal of Scripture. He must make it his responsibility to unite with the church that preaches the pure gospel of Christ, that properly administers the sacraments, that exercises discipline in love, and that holds to the headship of Christ. He must realize that the holiness of the church will be reflected by his own life. Moreover, regardless of the church in which providence has placed him, he must strive with heart, soul, mind, and strength to make the church approach the Holy Catholic Church portrayed in Scripture.

The individual church and denomination must strive after a corresponding visible expression of the unity, apostolicity, sanctity that marks the Holy Catholic Church. The ideal is the stature of the fulness of Christ. Striving for that ideal will hasten the unity of faith and holiness. Faith in the Holy Catholic Church should find a corresponding effort to the historical realization of the ideal.

Church".

I. BELIEVE

Chapter X

INVISIBLE AND VISIBLE

Corporate church union has become the strong passion of
many ecumenists. The church must be seen and grasped almost
as a material object. An organized oneness has become for some
almost the essence of Christianity. Unless the church exists in
some unified visible organization she will fail to impress the
world and fulfil the will of God. Others feel that a federation
of churches sufficiently accomplishes the ecumenical purpose.
Bishop Lesslie Newbigin expresses fear that the World Council
of Churches will give permanency to the idea of federation. He
writes, "As an organ of cooperation and conversation, the World
Council of Churches goes from strength to strength. But the
visible reunion of the Churches makes little progress, and indeed, denominational positions tend to harden. Thus the Council, instead of being something essentially transitional, tends
to appear more and more as the permanent form of the Churches'
unity. Its ecclesiological neutrality is in danger of becoming a
screen for ecclesiological federalism" (*The Household of God,*
p. 17).

More and more ecumenists accept the Roman Catholic position that visibility, as including one external organization, is an
essential property of the church. Quoting from Bishop Newbigin
again, "The Catholic rightly believes that it is of the nature of
the Church to be one visible fellowship, and if he is serious he
must believe that his own Church is that fellowship" (*ibid.,*

p. 16). In that same paragraph he points out how difficult it is for the Catholic to give up the conception that episcopacy is essential to the church. He adds, "Yet by sticking to it he is defending a vital Christian truth which would otherwise apparently go by default" (*ibid.*, p. 17). Evangelicals, while maintaining the existence of "a catholic visible church, consisting of all those throughout the world that profess that true religion, together with their children," deny the necessity of *one* organized ecclesiastical society that stands out visible to the eyes of men as the true church of God. This historic protestant position many are willing to jeopardize or sacrifice to achieve one organized structure for the church.

INVISIBLE

Someone has stated, "For the leaders of Ecumenicalism, the idea of the invisible church has been the opium of Christianity." The idea, however, originates with Scripture. The prophets constantly impressed the people that membership in the visible Israel did not qualify for the Israel of God. Men might enter into the visible Temple and have the visible sign of circumcision but only he who had clean hands, a pure heart, and spoke the truth in his heart, abode in the invisible tabernacle and holy place of God (Ps. 15:1, 2; 24:3, 4). The prophets spoke of a spiritual remnant within the external Israel (Ezra 9:8; Isa. 1:9; 10:21; Jer. 23:3; Ezek. 6:8). Elijah felt that all of Israel had apostatized and that he was the only true worshipper left; but God informed him that there were seven thousand who had not bowed the knee to Baal—invisible to man but visible to God. Paul gathers up the Old Testament teaching in Romans 2:28, 29 and 9:5, "For he is not a Jew, which is one outwardly; neither is that circumcision, which is outward in the flesh: but he is a Jew, which is one inwardly; and circumcision is that of the heart, in the spirit, and not in the letter. . . . For they are not all Israel, which are of Israel." Neither the prophets nor the apostles equated the outward Israel with the inward Israel. Whereas Scripture uses the terms *outward* and *inward, Israel after the flesh* and *Israel after the spirit.* Protestant theologians and creeds employ the terms *visible* and *invisible.*

Our Lord points up the same truth when he spoke harshly

to those who boasted that they were the children of Abraham, "Ye are of your father the devil, and the lusts of your father ye will do" (John 8:39-42). In the Sermon on the Mount he stated concerning those of the new dispensation, "Not every one that saith unto me, Lord, Lord, shall enter into the kingdom of heaven; but he that doeth the will of my Father which is in heaven. Many will say to me in that day, Lord, Lord, have we not prophesied in thy name? and in thy name have cast out devils? and in thy name done many wonderful works? And then will I profess unto them, I never knew you: depart from me ye that work iniquity" (Matt. 7:21-23). The unrighteous and unholy, though they may belong to the visible church, are excluded from the Israel of God, the New Jerusalem.

Based on Scriptures the creeds of the church have for the most part defined the invisible church and differentiated her from the visible. Typical is the definition of the Westminster Confession, chapter XXV, "The catholic or universal Church, which is invisible, consists of the whole number of the elect, that have been, are, or shall be gathered into one, under Christ the Head thereof; and is the spouse, the body, the fulness of him that filleth all in all." Any definition that does not take in the complete Church would not be descriptive of the catholic or universal Church. Any definition that would include all in the visible church, irrespective of belief or life, would not be descriptive of the *holy* catholic church. The composition of the invisible Church is given in Revelation 21:27, "And there shall in no wise enter into it anything that defileth, neither whatsoever worketh abomination, or maketh a lie: but they which are written in the Lamb's book of life."

Protestant theologians and creeds have stressed the conception of the invisible Church because the visible church presupposes the invisible and proceeds from it. Modern ecumenism would reverse that order as the Roman Catholic Church has done in the past. A Roman Catholic theologian, Möhler, contrasts Lutheranism and Catholicism thus—"The latter teaches that there is first the visible church, and then comes the invisible, whereas Protestantism affirms that out of the invisible comes the visible church, and the first is the ground of the last" (*Sybolic*, Sixth edition, Mainz, 1843). The church is born from above and not from below. The vertical line appears before the horizontal. The regenerating power of the Holy Spirit is antecedent to and the ground of the visible church. Paul expresses it thus, "But Jerusalem which is above is free, which is the Mother of us all" (Gal. 4:26). An angel indicated that he would show the apostle John the Bride, the Lamb's wife. He carried John to a great and high mount and showed him "that great city, the holy Jerusalem, descending out of heaven from God" (Rev. 21:10). While interpreters generally have thought of this as picturing the Church in heaven actually it depicts the Church as descending *out of heaven*. This, we feel, relates to the Church in history and not the eschatological Church. However, the fact stands out that the Church descends from heaven. The source of her growth, strength, beauty, and glory is situated in heaven and does not come from inherent grace deposited within the church to be passed on from generation to generation by a hierarchy. The river of grace proceeds from the throne of God and of the Lamb.

While the full concept of the invisible Church includes the redeemed of all ages, a narrower concept relates the church to the earth at a given time. To distinguish her from the Church in heaven the creeds have termed her by the name of Militant Church. While in a sense those who belong to the invisible Church on earth are visible yet only God knows those who are truly his. Man cannot determine or point out those who truly belong to Israel of God.

CHURCH CATHOLIC VISIBLE

In a second and broader aspect the church comprehends all professing Christians on earth at any given time. This has been termed the church catholic visible. The church in this sense consists of all those throughout the world that profess the true religion, together with their children. This is the world-wide church—the ecumenical church—that many would unite into one corporate church by including it under one organization.

The concept of an invisible and visible church upon earth does not imply that these are properly two churches, but one church contemplated in two different aspects—internal and external. The external church includes the invisible. The Bible and experience teach that the visible church includes in her membership those who do not properly belong. Hypocrites, heretics, and immoral men have entered into the visible church. Even the apostles could not restrain them as the reading of hearts belongs to God. While some may be removed through discipline as their evil becomes evident many are undiscerned. The present earthly church suffers from imperfections and cannot wholly repel evil admixtures.

How thankful Christians should be for the biblical and creedal concept of the invisible Church. Periods in history have gone by in which the visible church was sunk in corruption and ignorance. Think of the church in the dark ages and in the century previous to the Reformation. Evil existed within the church of which one can speak only with shame. In the period after the Reformation to this present day the visible church has not been unspotted by corruption and heresy. What the Lord revealed to the church in Sardis could make present day application, "Thou hast a name that thou livest, and art dead." Nevertheless, even during the most degrading period of church history the invisible church, consisting of those who love the Lord and perform his will, existed as the seven thousand who had not bowed the knee to Baal. Judging by outward appearances and looking upon the "visible" church, the assumption might well be in various periods of history that the gates of hell had prevailed against the church. However, the Lord preserved his own and time after time led them to purify and reform the visible church.

PARTICULAR CHURCHES

The church catholic visible consists of many denominations that are generally termed particular churches. One or many local churches may constitute a particular church. The relation of the particular church to the church catholic visible is well stated in the confession of the Polish Churches, the Declaratio Thorumensis, "There are particular Churches and the Church universal. The true universal Church is the community of all believers dispersed throughout the world, who are and remain one Catholic Church so long as they are united by subjection to one head, Christ, by the indwelling of one spirit, and the profession of the same faith; and this though they be not associated in one common external polity, but, as regards external fellowship and ecclesiastical regimen, be not in communion with each other. Particular Churches are societies of Christians who, besides being united by the internal bond of the Spirit, are under the same external polity. With respect to these, although they alone are true and living members of the Church who are united to Christ by faith and to Christ's body, not only externally but internally, yet, since the spiritual fellowship of Christians is a thing invisible, all who remain in visible communion with the Church are, in the judgment of charity, to be esteemed members thereof, although many of them may, in the sight of God, be hypocrites. A true particular Church is distinguished from a false one by the profession of the true faith, the unmutilated administration of the Sacraments, and the exercise of discipline: all other notes are accidental and subordinate."

The charge gains ground that existence of particular churches (denominations) constitutes sin and harms the witness of Christianity. Dr. Morrison writes, "Modern Protestantism is in bondage to the denominational system which has stripped the church catholic of the organs and functions by which it could manifest its true nature as the Church of Christ" and "Our separate denominations have assumed that they could bear witness to the whole gospel of Christ. But now our eyes are being opened to the truth that only the whole church, acting as a united whole, can bear witness to the whole gospel" (*The Unfinished Reformation*, pp. 23, 24). In repudiating the idea of a federation of churches, Bishop Newbigin stated, "They do not grapple with the fact, which any serious reading of the New Testament must surely make inescapable, that to speak of a plurality of Churches is strictly absurd; that we can only do so insofar as we have ceased to understand by the word 'Church' what the New Testament means by it; that our ecclesiologies are, in the Pauline sense, carnal" (1 Cor. 3:3-4) (*The Household of God*, p. 14).

Neither Dr. Morrison nor Bishop Newbigin seem to understand the relation of the local or particular church to the church catholic visible. Every particular church has the name, attributes, sacraments, revealed oracles, and responsibilities of the church catholic. If a particular church does not have the marks of the church catholic it ceases to be a church and becomes a synagogue of Satan. Surely the promise of Jesus, "Where two or three are gathered in my name there am I in their midst," applies to a local or particular church as well as the church catholic. Christ commanded John to write a message in a book and send it "unto the seven churches which are in Asia" (Rev. 1:11); each of these had separate organizations to impose discipline and apparently there existed no hierarchy or central organization for these churches in Asia. The concept of *church* and *churches* is not foreign to the New Testament.

What from one point of view appears as a number of separate components may from another view be regarded as an organic entity. What is common to the many elements is fundamental and connective—Christ, the Spirit, the written Word, the ministry, and sacraments. Not only the written Word but the creeds have emphasized the above as the important and fundamental cohesives. The Savoy Declaration of Congregational Churches in England (1658) states, "Unto this catholic visible Church Christ hath given the ministry, oracles, and ordinances of God, for the gathering and perfecting of the saints, in this life, to the end of the world; and doth by his own presence and Spirit, according to his promise, make them effectual thereunto. This catholic Church hath been sometimes more, sometimes less visible. And particular churches, which are members thereof, are more or less pure, according as the doctrine of the gospel is taught and embraced, ordinances administered, and public worship performed more or less purely in them." That is, common to both catholic church and particular church are the ministry, oracles, ordinances, and presence of Christ and his Spirit.

CHURCH VISIBILITY

What gives visibility to the Church of Jesus Christ? The first and obvious answer is—the membership. Yet the membership cannot be assembled in one place so that the world may see the "visible" church. Nor may a representative body of the aggregate membership entitle itself as the "visible" church for it is at the most a partial representation. Nor could a central organization, located in some prominent city, entitle itself as the "visible" church. Yet that is for what some ecumenists are pressing to give the church visibility. And surely having one name does not give scriptural visibility for the church is more than just a name.

The creeds stress that the visible church is seen where the Gospel is rightly taught, the sacraments rightly administered, and discipline exercised. The Nineteenth Article of the Confession of the Church of England declares, "The visible Church of Christ is a congregation of faithful men, in which the pure Word of God is preached, and the Sacraments be duly ministered according to Christ's ordinance, in all these things that of necessity are required to do the same." What an impression it would make on the world if in every hamlet, town, and city of the world the gospel were preached in its purity! This would impress the world far more than a unified organization with churches preaching and teaching a dozen varieties of gospels. Add to the preaching of the true gospel the right administration of the sacraments and the exercise of scriptural discipline, then the visibility of the church would be impressive throughout the world. But, alas, the minds of men are occupied with lesser and outward forms of unity.

Not only preaching of the pure Word of God, proper administration of the sacraments, and biblical discipline give visibility to the church, but also true holiness exhibited in the believer's life. The life must conform to the message. To the outside world a righteous life is the best norm of judging the effectiveness of Christianity and usefulness of the church. The pagan reaches this conclusion, "If their works are better than mine, their faith must be better than mine." Jesus said, "By this shall all men know that ye are my disciples, if ye have love one to another" (John 13:35). In the first century of Christianity the words of our Lord were very remarkably verified. The church became visible to the eyes of the heathen who were led to exclaim, "See how these Christians love one another and how ready they are to die for each other!" The profane Lucian scoffingly says of the Christians of his day, "Their Law-giver has persuaded them that they are all brethren." This illustrates how genuine and mutual affection among Christians gave visibility to the church.

We have great cause to lament that love is a minus quantity

in twentieth century religious life and not so visible as in the primitive age. The church has lost to a great degree the glory of dynamic love. This is also true in some degree of other Christian virtues. Solidarity of family life, honesty, purity, truthfulness, generosity and unselfishness are characteristics that have given a glorious visibility seen of all men. Their absence dims the glory of the church upon earth.

Instead of the cliché of the old liberals, "not creed, but life," the church may well adopt the slogan, "not organization, but life," if she desires to become visible to the world. The church has discovered to her sorrow that one cannot have life without creed even as the Israelites in bondage could not make brick without straw. During the time of the Reformation the church discovered that one could have organization without truth and life. For her fullest glory and greatest visibility the church should display all the marks of the Holy Catholic Church. These consist of the preaching of the pure gospel, proper administration of the sacraments, exercise of biblical discipline, and conformity of life to message. Then and only then will the brightness of her glory be witnessed in the world.

Chapter XI

THE BODY OF CHRIST

Those who speak of denominationalism as dismembering and fragmenting the body of Christ show abysmal ignorance of the biblical significance of this figure of speech. They conceive that the term applies to visible organization without which the body of Christ does not and cannot exist as a whole. If this be true— if visibility, as including one external organization, is of the essence of the body—then unity of the body can never be achieved or manifested upon earth because the Head remains invisible. No wonder that the Roman Catholic Church, which insists on visibility as an essential property of the Church, has a visible vicar to represent Christ. Those who insist that the figure *body* expresses a visible, material concept rather than mystical and spiritual separate the head from the body. While they may not feel guilty of splintering and fragmenting the body of Christ they succeed in severing the Head from the body.

BASIC SCRIPTURE PASSAGES

The study of scriptural passages from which the figure of speech is taken will reveal that the underlying thought behind the figure is to show a spiritual relationship between Christ and believers. Dependence upon Christ receives emphasis in the figure while the thought of a visible structure does not appear. The body receives life from the Head. Members of the body have union together not through an external organization instituted by Christ but by virtue of their union with him. That is, Christ is both the vertical and horizontal bond of unity. Organizational unity receives little or no attention in the New Testament because it would tend to hide the stronger, deeper, more lasting bond—Christ Jesus. This becomes very apparent in the following passages where in the figure predominates:

> So we, being many, are one body in Christ, and every one members one of another (Rom. 12:5).

> For as the body is one, and hath many members, and all the members of that one body, being many, are one body: so also is Christ. For by one Spirit are we all baptized into one body. . . . Now ye are the body of Christ, and members in particular (1 Cor. 12:12, 13, 27).

> And he is the head of the body, the church: who is the beginning, the first-born from the dead: that in all things he might have the preeminence. . . . And not holding the Head, from which the body by joints and bands having nourishment ministered and knit together increaseth with the increase of God (Col. 1:18; 2:19).

> And hath put all things under his feet, and given him to be the head over all things to the church, which is his body, the fulness of him that filleth all in all. . . . There is one body. . . . for the edifying of the body of Christ. . . . From whom the whole body fitly joined together and compacted by that which every joint supplieth according to the effectual working in the measure of every part, maketh increase of the body unto the edifying of itself in love. . . . For the husband is the head of the wife, even as Christ is the head of the church: and he is the saviour of the body. . . . For we are members of his body, of his flesh, and of his bones (Eph. 1:22, 23; 4:4, 16; 5:23, 30).

A number of rather clear impressions are conveyed by the apostle Paul in these passages. First, the body of Christ exists as an organic whole; second, the figure is employed to stress the relationship of Christ to the Church; third, the body comes into being through Christ; fourth, body receives its unity through union with Christ; and fifth, the concept is spiritual.

Even a cursory reading of the passages conveys the thought that the body exists as an organic whole—*we, being many, are one body; there is one body; as the body is one; by one Spirit are we all baptized into one body; now ye are the body of Christ.* Most scholars agree that an overall organization did not exist in the first century church; yet the apostle teaches clearly that one body did exist. Because individual or groups of churches have separate organizations does not imply a fragmentation of the body of Christ. Paul also uses the figure of the temple to indicate the organic oneness of the Church, "In whom all the building fitly framed together groweth unto an holy temple in the Lord: in whom ye also are builded together for an habitation of God through the Spirit" (Eph. 2:21, 22). The fundamental idea of this text is that the Church constitutes an organic totality. The possibility of a fragmented body because of separate organizations is an absurd idea as one grasps the fundamental significance of the figure used by Paul.

The second impression the quoted passages convey is that the term *body* focuses special attention to the Head. Even as the focal point of interest of the human body is the head even so the head of the spiritual body receives particular attention. This receives emphasis in Colossians 1:18, "He is the head of the body, the church . . . that in all things he might have the preeminence." This concept humbles man who conceives himself to be the center of the universe. Man is not the head but the body and exists to give glory to the Head. In the fourth chapter of Revelation the Church casts crowns before the throne saying, "Thou art worthy, O Lord, to receive glory and honour and power: for thou hast created all things, and for thy pleasure they are and were created." Both the old and new creation came into existence for the glory of God and by the decree of the Father, Christ is to have preeminence in all things. God has purposed to gather together in one all things in Christ, whether in heaven or upon earth, Ephesians 1:10. Even evangelicals are prone to think that the primary object of the Gospel is the salvation of man. The Scriptures, however, indicate rather clearly that the creation of the Church was for the glory of God and in this dispensation the glory is to be focused on the Lord Jesus Christ. Christ is the Head of the body, the church.

A third clear idea gleaned from the passages referring to the concept of body is that the body receives life from the Head. He is the saviour of the body. As Eve was formed from Adam so "we are members of his body, of his flesh, and of his bones." As branches receive life from the vine so the body receives life from Christ. The Church is the creation of Christ. The Church is born from above. Christ is that Bread upon which the Church lives. The Church receives life by eating his flesh and drinking his blood. Christ caused the Church to rise from a death in trespasses and sin. Because Christ lives the Church lives also. Christ entered into the world that the Church might have life and might have it more abundantly. Without the Head there is no Church. Without the Head the body dies.

Important for present day study on the nature of unity is the concept taught by the indicated passages that the body achieves unity through union with Christ. Because the Church is one body in Christ, believers become members one of another. "We, being many, are one body in Christ, and every one members one of another." The body is knit together by the Head. From Christ the whole body is fitly joined together. Paul's conception of unity is not related to polity but is ontologically motivated—unity belongs to the very essence of the Church. The Church is conceived as a collective personality. Unity exists —otherwise the body does not exist. Unity is not contingent on organization but on union with Christ. To speak of union with Christ and a fragmented body is an absurdity and insults Christ who knits together and joins together those who are his. Christ supplies the Spirit by which all believers are baptized into one body. Those who speak about the fragmentation of the body of Christ speak about a monstrosity that exists only in the minds of those who have failed to grasp the biblical figure of speech.

The fifth impression from the quoted passages is that the concept of body is spiritual, "for by one Spirit are we all baptized into one body." Some ecumenists maintain that the "body" is the visible church upon earth, especially the one that shows continuity through the historic episcopate. The root error of that position is that it equates the visible church with the spiritual body of Christ. We know that the visible church contains dead members who do not belong to the living organism —the body of Christ. There are those within the church on earth to whom Christ will say, "I never knew you: depart from me, ye that work iniquity." The tares and the bad fish (Matt. 13) never were in vital relationship to Christ. They were not members of that body of which Christ is declared the saviour. They were not members of his body, of his flesh, and of his bones. As one studies the passages in which the figure of speech appears he realizes that he is in the sphere of the spiritual. Totally absent from these passages is the concept of organizational structure or a continuation of life through an episcopate. The true Church is a mystical, spiritual body, whereof Christ is the Head.

SIGNIFICANCE OF BODY

The human body forms an excellent analogy since it illustrates the organic unity of the Church. The wonderful structure of the body, consisting of many different members, united in one frame, each necessary for the perfection and good of the whole and animated by one living principle, makes the body an apt figure of speech for the apostle Paul who uses it frequently. He writes, "For as the body is one, and hath many members, and all the members of that one body, being many, are one body: so also is Christ" (1 Cor. 12:12). A body consists of many parts but there is in it an essential unity—even so the Church. In the same chapter of Corinthians Paul shows the importance of every member to the body and that the diversity of gifts contributes to the glory and usefulness of the body.

The employment of the term *body* indicates a far more intimate relationship between believers than members of an external ecclesiastical organization. Paul writes, "And whether one member suffer, all members suffer with it; or one member be honoured, all members rejoice with it" (1 Cor. 12:26). The sympathy of the whole church extends to such members who may be in the midst of persecution for truth's sake, who may be in deep sorrow or who may be in bodily affliction. Envy does not rise at a brother's advancement. The church rejoices with them that rejoice and weeps with them that weep. The Head also closely associates himself with the body as he reveals, "Verily I say unto you, inasmuch as ye have done it unto one of the least of these my brethren, ye have done it unto me"

(Matt. 25:40). No human organization can match the close relationship that exists within the body of Christ.

Paul uses the similitude of a body to denote also that the body receives nourishment and increase from the Head. "And not holding the Head, from which the body by joints and bands having nourishment ministered and knit together increaseth with the increase of God" (Col. 2:19; cf. Eph. 4:16). As the head supplies nourishment that gives life and strength to all parts of the body, so Christ supplies nourishment to all members of his Church. Upon this nourishment depend the glory, growth and increase of the body. Each member receives grace for holiness and obedience, without which he would become a withered and dead branch. Strength, purity, blessedness, joy, love and peace are communicated by Christ. Whatever power the church possesses has come as a gift from the King. He gives life and the more abundant life. The body testifies, "I am crucified with Christ: nevertheless I live; yet not I, but Christ liveth in me: and the life which I now live in the flesh I live by the faith of the Son of God, who loved me, and gave himself for me" (Gal. 2:20). Spiritual life finds its source in Christ and is maintained by Christ.

An efficient and unified organization has been stressed as a means to greater growth and influence for the church. The Scriptures stress that increase of the body depends on a closer union with Christ. Human means are inadequate in the fight against the power of darkness. Mere organization cannot convert the human soul and release it from the power of Satan. The church must depend upon supernatural power and that can only be obtained from Christ. As far as the increase of the church is concerned the incorporation of various denominations into one corporate body will avail little or nothing. Mergers of denominations have not demonstrated that growth results. The great and primary effort should be to incorporate the membership into Christ. With the life of Christ flowing into the churches the increase will take care of itself. The church cannot have either life or growth if she does not have a vital union with Christ.

HEADSHIP OF CHRIST

More than sympathy with the body and nourishment of it is involved in the headship of Christ. As the human body is subject to the head so the Church is subject to Christ. The apostle informs us that "the head of every man is Christ" (1 Cor. 11:3), and that the rule of a husband over his wife finds illustration in the rule of Christ over the Church (Eph. 5:22-24). Never must the fact be lost sight of that the Church is the body *of Christ*. He purchased her with his precious blood. God gave the Church into the possession of the Son as a reward for his perfect obedience. The Church is a jealous possession of Christ who will not share his headship with any human vicar or hierarchy. He requires no deputy, "For where two or three are gathered together in my name, there am I in the midst of them." While it is true that he delegates certain powers and responsibilities to the ministry, he does not delegate his headship. Ministers are servants within his house and not lords. They obey his bidding and carry out his commandments. They, as well as the entire church, are subject to him.

In the natural body the head is the seat of intelligence and the will. The head plans, directs and controls the members of the body. The body obeys and executes the designs of the head. Even so Christ plans, directs and controls while the Church renders obedience. Christ has given his laws, rules, precepts, and doctrines and recorded them in Scripture. In his commission to the apostles (Matt. 28:19, 20) all nations were commanded "to observe all things whatsoever I have commanded you." He brooks no interference. Those who teach contrary to his instructions and precepts are false apostles and harm the life and growth of the church. There is nothing in the church that is not subject to his teachings and directives.

The verses previous to Colossians 1:18, where Christ is indicated as head of the body, give the ground and qualification of his headship. The ground is that "we have redemption through his blood, even the forgiveness of sins" (vs. 14). He is eminently qualified, " for by him were all things created, that are in heaven, and that are in earth, visible and invisible, whether they be thrones, or dominions, or principalities, or powers: all things were created by him, and for him: and he is before all things, and by him all things consist" (vss. 16, 17). The same qualification is given in Ephesians 1:22, "And hath put all things under his feet, and gave him to be the head over all things to the church." It is not difficult to render obedience to the King of kings and the Lord of lords. The comfort and the hope of the Church in fulfilling her mission lies in the fact that both the church and universe are under Christ's administration. Because all power has been given to him both in heaven and upon earth the church can go forward conquering and to conquer.

RELATION TO VISIBLE CHURCH

What is declared about the body of Christ in Scriptures cannot be identified with the entire visible church upon earth. Those who maintain that all baptized members of the visible church form the body of Christ ignore the biblical distinction between the invisible and visible church (see Chapter X). Bishop Newbigin protests this distinction as he tries to establish the paradox of sin and holiness in the believer to be the paradox of the visible church. "That paradox, familiar to every Christian is perhaps the simplest way of expressing the paradox of the Church's being" (*The Household of God*, p. 143). He maintains that Luther's doctrine of justification by faith for the individual should be applied to the corporate, visible church. He writes, "But if this is true, then Luther abandoned his deepest insight when he substituted for the true, biblical picture of a Church both holy and sinful, a false and unbiblical distinction between the spiritual church and the material Church or between the invisible Church and the visible Church. Both of these related pairs of terms have the effect of relaxing the true eschatological tension which is involved in recognizing that in Christ we, along with all our brethren, are accepted as His while we are yet sinners, and of substituting an essentially legalistic and pharisaic conception that some are—so to say—in the Church by right and others only by grace" (*ibid.* p. 143).

What Bishop Newbigin implies is that the visible church is saved in its entirety. Those who receive the external rites of the church are *ipso facto* members of the body of Christ. It is a known fact that within the visible church there are those who deny the fundamental doctrines of the Christian faith and those who live immoral lives. Paul speaks pointedly to the Corinthian church, "Know ye not that the unrighteous shall not inherit the kingdom of God" (1 Cor. 6:9). Jesus in the Sermon on the Mount denies entrance to the Kingdom to those who had not lived according to the will of God though they had made profession of faith. As Paul states in the eighth chapter of Romans, "Now if any man have not the Spirit of Christ, he is none of his." Neither Christ nor the apostles equate the visible church with the body of Christ.

Some hold the position that our incorporation in Christ is by faith while our incorporation into the body of Christ is by baptism and maintained by partaking of the sacrament of the Lord's Supper. The Scriptures, however, teach that by virtue of being in Christ through faith we are incorporated into his body. It is by the Spirit that we are all baptized into one body (1 Cor. 12:13) and not by the external act of baptism. By baptism we enter into the visible church. The external rite of baptism recognizes that through faith we have been incorporated into the body of Christ. And those who are truly in the body of Christ are subject to him and dependent upon him. They participate in his life and are animated by his Spirit. It is altogether possible that one may be baptized and partake of the Lord's Supper and be entirely devoid of such spiritual life that comes by virtue of union with Christ.

THE ONE AND THE MANY

What greatly concerns ecumenists is how to reconcile the conception of the one body of Christ with the existence of different church bodies. The prevalence of many denominations, they feel, precludes the church of Christ from presenting the whole gospel. Dr. Morrison writes, "But now our eyes are being opened to the truth that only the whole church, acting as a united whole, can bear witness to the whole gospel" (*The Unfinished Reformation,* p. 24). The idea persists that as long as individual churches and denominations are not within one corporate framework, they cannot properly function as the body of Christ. A fragment of the body, they reason, cannot perform as effectively as the entire body. A plurality of churches cannot operate as efficiently and powerfully as one church body. They even assert that the existence of many church organizations handicaps the work of the Holy Spirit. However, the Holy Spirit did work powerfully in the primitive church although there was no uniform organization. The early church was not disturbed by the plurality of churches that is of so much concern to so many in the 20th century church. The reason for this is that the primitive church, under the instruction of the apostles, understood the relation between the one and the many.

The relation of a particular church to the body of Christ may be seen in a study of 1 Corinthians 12 where the figure of speech predominates. Throughout the chapter Paul writes as though he is referring to the universal church—"For by one Spirit are we all baptized into one body" (vs. 13). Yet he concludes with the remark, "Now ye are the body of Christ, and members in particular" (vs. 27). He says, as it were, all that I have described of the universal church, holds true of the Corinthian church. Each individual church has the attributes of the universal and can be described, as Paul does, to be the body of Christ. The Corinthian church was not a fragment or splinter. Paul said, "Ye are the body of Christ."

Christ is as much the Head of a particular church or denomination as he is of the Church catholic visible. Where two or three are gathered in his name there is he in their midst even as much as if the whole church were gathered together. It does not require the gathering of the entire visible church to administer the sacraments properly or to proclaim the whole counsel of God. This can be done within one congregation. Thank God the relation of Christ to the church does not depend upon the existence of one organization! It depends upon his grace and the presence of his Spirit.

The very use of the term body indicates that the church is not a mere organization, institution or corporation but an organism in vital relationship to the Head. There is a real intimate and living union between Christ and his Church. Because of union with Christ unity is an essential characteristic of the Church although she may exist in many distinct denominations. "The Church," says Cyprian, "is one which by reason of its fecundity is extended into a multitude, in the same manner as the rays of the sun, however numerous, constitute but one light; and the branches of a tree, however many, are attached to one trunk, which is supported by its tenacious root; and when various rivers flow from the same fountain, though number is diffused by the redundant supply of waters, unity is preserved in their origin." Christ is the Fountain from which many healing streams flow; Christ is the Vine from which fruitful branches grow; Christ is the Light from which lesser lights shine before men.

The concept of the body as presented in Scripture must be wonderfully comforting to isolated groups of Christians in such lands as communist Russia and China. Under the concept of some ecumenists they would be dismembered fragments of the body of Christ because cut off from organizational unity with the church in free countries. Reading the Scriptures, however, they know that they form the body of Christ and are in living relationship to the Head. Who dares to divide the unity of God in Christ? Who shall separate them from the body of Christ?

Chapter XII

THE LIVING TEMPLE

Of great significance to the problem of church and world unity is the Temple of ancient Israel. Both Old and New Testament writers viewed the Temple as the institution through which God would establish unity and peace throughout the world. No ecumenical study can be complete without understanding the message of hope that the Temple has for the church and the world. As people become disillusioned with the United Nations as the final answer to unity and peace of the world, they should be informed vigorously that the Word of God reveals the unifying force that will cause the lion and the lamb to lie down together. The church, instead of concentrating on building up the United Nations as the institution ordained of God to bring harmony, should concentrate on rebuilding the Temple of the living God.

The Temple was the center of unity for the Jew. It constituted the very heart and center of worship. Even in distant lands, during times of captivity, the Jew worshipped God with his face towards the holy Temple. Those who settled in heathen lands would make long and arduous pilgrimages so that they could worship their God within the walls of the holy city, Jerusalem. The worship of the Temple bound the hearts of the Jews together and made the bonds of unity so strong that even two thousand years after the destruction of the Temple the Jewish race witnesses a solidarity that is a constant wonder in the world. Common worship shows its cohesive power even to the thousandth generation. The answer to the problem of unity is not a diversified worship, but identical worship. The answer to the problem of world unity is a common center of worship.

The Temple, according to the Prophets, was not only to be the center of unity for Israel but for the entire world. Both Isaiah and Micah record this glorious prophecy:

> And it shall come to pass in the last days, that the mountain of the Lord's house shall be established in the top of the mountains, and shall be exalted above the hills; and all nations shall flow unto it. And many people shall go and say, Come ye, and let us go up to the mountain of the Lord, to the house of the God of Jacob; and he will teach us of his ways, and we will walk in his paths; for out of Zion shall go forth the law, and the word of the Lord from Jerusalem. And he shall judge among the nations, and shall rebuke many people: and they shall beat their swords into plowshares, and their spears into pruninghooks: nation shall not lift up sword against nation, neither shall they learn war any more (Isaiah 2:2-4).

The Prophet looked forward to the time of the Messiah when the Temple would be established as the center of worship, revelation of the Word of the Lord would be accepted by all nations and the Headship of Christ be acknowledged. Unity, according to Isaiah, would be established by a common worship, common acceptance of the law, and headship of Christ. Diversity of worship and faith is foreign to the prophetic view.

Basic to the unity of Israel, and prophetically of the world, is the unity of God himself. Moses declared, "Hear, O Israel: the Lord our God is one Lord" (Deut. 6:4). The fact that the Temple could not be duplicated and multiplied taught the Jews that the Lord their God was one. A plurality of gods cannot establish unity. In their immature state of religious development the Israelites might have been led to believe in more than one god by the establishment of several places of temple worship but the existence of but one Temple prevented that. The Jews became a united people because they believed in one God. The world needs to hear the prophetic word of Moses, "Hear, O world, the Lord our God is one Lord." There is no basis of unity and peace without acceptance of it. This, too, the world will learn through the establishment of the one Temple as revealed in the New Testament.

The Temple spoke eloquently of the sublime truth that God was present with his people. His throne was in the holy of holies and his glory filled the temple. It echoed the wonderful truth of the covenant revealed to Abraham, "I will be a God to thee, and to thy seed after thee." His presence assured the people of favor and protection. That this covenant promise was not limited to the Jews is indicated by the court of Gentiles within the confines of the Temple. The ecumenical outreach has prominence in the Abrahamic convenant in the promise, "and in thee shall all the families of the earth be blessed." The Temple may be said to be a visible pledge of God's convenant relation to Israel and beyond them to all the families of earth that would embrace the covenant. Further, from the Temple proceeded the oracles and revelation of God.

Expressive as the Temple was of the blessing of God dwelling with his people even more vividly did it express the way by which the manifestation of God was obtained. The meeting of God with his people in the Temple was due to one fact, that there was instituted in it a blood-sprinkled mercy seat upon which he dwelt between the cherubim. The whole Temple with its furnishings and its ritual summoned attention to the glorious truth that remission of sins was obtained through the shedding of blood, not of the sinner, but of a substitute. The multitude of sacrifices indicated how sinful men could approach the holy God without fear and enjoy communion with him forever. The blood-sprinkled mercy seat declared propitiation and sinful man could enter into the very presence of the holy God to receive his favor. Thus the ancient Temple gave eloquent witness that the love of God had provided the means through which his holiness was vindicated and his justice satisfied and all that entered the Temple would experience the favor of God.

The prophets indicated that the message of the Temple would be proclaimed to all mankind. We have already referred to Isaiah 2:2-4 which declares that all nations would flow to the House of God that they might learn his ways and walk in his paths. And the Temple of the Lord would declare to them the one way by which they could walk in his paths—through acceptance of the sacrifice for sin. Isaiah later points out that the Suffering Servant would be that sacrifice, wounded for our transgressions and bruised for our iniquity (Is. 53). And on the basis of that substitutionary sacrifice the Lord says of strangers to the commonwealth of Israel, "Even them will I bring to my holy mountain and make them joyful in my house of prayer: their burnt-offerings and their sacrifices shall be accepted upon mine altar; for mine house shall be called an house of prayer for all people" (Isa. 56:7). The prophet Jeremiah proclaims the same message, "At that time they shall call Jerusalem the throne of the Lord; and all the nations shall be gathered unto it, to the name of the Lord, to Jerusalem" (Jere. 3:17). (cf. Zech. 8:20 ff.; 14:16). Malachi indicates that this is prophetic of more than a material temple located in Palestine, in these words, "From the rising of the sun even unto the going down of the same my name shall be great among the Gentiles; and in every place incense shall be offered unto my name, and a pure offering: for my name shall be great among the heathen, saith the Lord of hosts" (Mal. 1:11). The New Testament, of course, fills in the scope and nature of the living Temple of which the earthly Temple was a type and shadow. Sufficient has been shown that the prophets looked forward to the time when all mankind would have one common Temple, a common center of worship, and would thereby be formed into a unity.

NEW TESTAMENT FULFILMENT

In connection with the cleansing of the Temple at the beginning of his ministry, Jesus spoke a word that lodged tenaciously in the minds of the Jews so that we find them referring to it in his trial before the Sanhedrin (Matt. 26:61; Mark 14:58), flinging it in his face at Calvary (Mark 15:29), and echoing it at the trial of Stephen (Acts 6:13, 14). In answer for a sign demanding his authority for cleansing the Temple, Jesus said, "Destroy this temple, and in three days I will raise it up. . . . But he spake of the temple of his body" (John 2:19, 21). Commentators, in the main, have done scant justice to the import of Christ's comparing his body to the Temple. Christ's body is the antitype of the Temple. As God declared the Temple to be his dwelling place, so in Christ dwelleth the fulness of the Godhead bodily; as the Temple was the meeting place, where sinners found God at the mercy seat, so in the crucified Christ, God is to be found reconciled with sinners; as the Temple was the place from which the oracles of God proceeded, so Christ is to be heard in the revelation of the Father and his will. As the ancient Temple gave visible witness that the love of God had provided the means through which his holiness was vindicated and his justice satisfied, so the broken body of Christ (the temple destroyed) gives visible witness that the love of God has provided the sacrifice whereby his holiness is vindicated and his justice satisfied. The Jews, blind to the truth the Temple represented and deaf to its message, did not know that He spoke of the temple of his body. They did not know that "one greater than the temple is here" (Matt. 12:6). The very structure, frame, constitution and design of the original Temple pointed to the work and person of the Messiah.

The material Temple is now replaced by the person of Christ. Worship, which found its center in the ancient Temple, finds it in Christ. Unity which emanated from the Temple now emanates from Christ. The bond of unity, strengthened by worship within the Temple, finds its strength in the worship of Christ. The hope for peace within this world is found only in the Prince of peace. The solidarity that amazed the first century found its cohesion in Christ. In the apocalyptic vision the apostle John says, "And I saw no temple therein; for the Lord God Almighty and the Lamb are the temple of it." No material temple exists today nor is there any need: the Lamb, who is the Lord God Almighty, is the Temple.

In reference to his body Jesus said, "Destroy this temple, and in three days I will raise it up." This was prophetic of his bodily resurrection. But also this was prophetic of the raising of a new Israel and a new Temple. The people of the new dispensation are known as the body of Christ (cf Chapter XI). Based on his atonement a new living Temple displaces the old material Temple. The Temple of Jerusalem is displaced by the universal Temple of prophecy. The classical passage declaring this truth is Ephesians 2:19-22,

Now therefore ye are no more strangers and foreigners, but fellow-citizens with the saints, and of the household of God; and are built upon the foundation of the apostles and prophets, Jesus Christ himself being the chief corner stone; in whom all the building fitly framed together groweth unto an holy temple in the Lord: in whom ye also are builded together for and habitation of God through the Spirit.

Just previous to the above passage, Paul declares that those who were far off were made nigh, "by the blood of Christ" (vs. 13); and that Christ reconciled both Jew and Gentile "unto God in one body by the cross" (vs. 16). The foundation of the new Temple is the blood of Christ, the cross of Christ. Those who seek to rear an ecclesiastical structure on any other foundation are building upon sand. As in the old Temple the substitutionary sacrifice was basic to worship so in the Temple not built with hands. Only by the blood of Christ can God be approached and only by the cross of Christ is there reconciliation.

In the passage quoted above Jesus is termed the chief corner stone. There are so many facets to the person and work of Christ that we must expect different figures of speech. Thus Jesus can be called both the Temple under one aspect and the chief corner stone under another. (Eclectic and synthetic man with his finite mind tries to subsume revelation under one category such as incarnation, atonement, fatherhood, sovereignty, kingdom, church, christology, etc. Scripture, however, does not seek to mould revelation into one category.) The place of Jesus is interpreted by Isaiah, "Behold I lay in Zion for a foundation a stone, a tried stone, a precious corner stone, a sure foundation" (Isa. 28:16). By union with the corner stone, other stones are held in place, are fitly framed together and grow into a holy temple in the Lord.

Another facet of the work of Christ employs a different figure of speech—the builder of the temple. Prophetically Zechariah brings this to light, "Thus speaketh the Lord of hosts, saying, Behold, the man whose name is the BRANCH; and he shall grow up out of his place, and he shall build the temple of the Lord; even he shall build the temple of the Lord; and he shall bear the glory, and shall sit and rule upon his throne: and he shall be a priest upon his throne" (Zech. 6:12, 13). Even here we are reminded of the atonement in that the Messiah will be a priest upon his throne. That in Zechariah's prophecy the Messiah is prophesied as the builder reveals that more than the restoration of the material temple is indicated: the great living Temple that the Messiah would extend by the communication of his Spirit to the ends of the earth. Those who were far off would become living stones of that mystical Temple. Jesus points to the fulfilment of that prophecy in his statement to Peter, "I will build my church."

The material with which the Lord builds the Temple is earthy, carnal and sinful. By his touch, however, the dead stones are transformed into living stones. "Ye also, as lively stones, are built up a spiritual house, an holy priesthood, to offer up spiritual sacrifices, acceptable to God by Jesus Christ" (1 Pet. 2:5). The same power that raised Christ from the dead is exercised on behalf of those dead in trespasses and sin. They are regenerated by the power of the Spirit and form the living Temple upon earth. The building of the Temple cannot be accomplished except as Christ sends the Spirit with his quickening power.

Moreover, Christ is the architect of the building. One dare not modify his plans, including the edifice being "built upon the foundation of the apostles and prophets, Jesus Christ himself being the chief corner stone." That the apostles and prophets were to be the foundation indicated that revelation was given to them as to the design of the Temple. As care was taken with both the Tabernacle and Temple in that the pattern was shown to Moses and Solomon, one need not suppose that the structure of the living Temple was left to be designed by men. Moses was instructed, "And thou shalt rear up the tabernacle according to the fashion thereof which was shewed thee in the mount" (Exod. 26:30). David in his instruction to his son, Solomon, gave him the pattern for the Temple and 1 Chronicles 28:19 records, "All this, said David, the Lord made me understand in writing by his hand upon me, even all the works of this pattern." The instruction given to the twentieth century builders is that the Temple should conform to the teachings of the prophets and apostles. In other words, the living Temple must be apostolic.

THE ONE AND THE MANY

Christ takes on the several parts of being the Temple, its sacrifice, and its builder. By virtue of these distinct capacities, he gives rise to multifold temples. These temples are adumbrations of the original, Christ Jesus. Undoubtedly, the Son of man was the heavenly pattern seen by Moses and translated into material concepts in the Tabernacle and Temple. By being conformed to the image of the Son, individual and community temples appear. 1 Corinthians 6:19 speaks of the individual believer being the temple, "What? know ye not that your body is the temple of the Holy Ghost which is in you, which ye have of God, and ye are not your own?" In 1 Corinthians 6:16 the community appears as the temple, "And what agreement hath the temple of God with idols? for ye are the temple of the living God; as God hath said, I will dwell in them, and walk in them; and I will be their God, and they shall by my people."

That the name of the temple is placed upon an individual, a community, and the total church need not trouble us. The believer is a multiform creature. In respect to God he is a temple in which the Holy Spirit is pleased to dwell; in respect to fellow Christians he is a living stone, conjoined by the same Spirit. A community of believers may be spoken of as the Temple of the living God; yet in relationship to the universal Church it is but a part. Some ecumenists have difficulty in understanding the biblical concept and feel that a uniform organization alone will manifest a complete Temple upon earth. They fail to grasp that the Temple is an organism and not an organization. They fail to comprehend the concept of the one and the many.

THE TEMPLE AND ECUMENISM

As Solomon's Temple, the antitype Christ Jesus and the ecumenical movement come to comparative view, a striking contrast is manifest: two witness the approach to God through substitutionary sacrifice; the third remains almost totally silent. The ancient Temple gives eloquent witness that the sinning Israelite meets God only at the blood-sprinkled mercy seat. Christ witnesses that except one drinks his blood there is no spiritual life, John 6:53. He gave his disciples the passover cup with the words, "For this is my blood of the new testament, which is shed for many for the remission of sin" (Matt. 26:28). Yet, with but an exceptional voice here and there, the ecumenical movement remains silent on the significance of Christ's blood for reconciliation to God and among men.

The scandal of the ecumenical movement is ignoring the blood of Christ as the means by which men are reconciled to God and brought into unity one with another.

How can the ecumenical movement ignore, what the Scriptures so clearly reveal, that the blessings of mankind come by virtue of the shed blood of Christ? The New Testament is rich with that truth: "the church purchased with his own blood" (Acts 20:28); "propitiation through faith in his blood" (Rom. 3:25); "justified by his blood" (Rom. 5:9); "communion of the blood of Christ" (1 Cor. 10:16); "redemption through his blood" (Eph. 1:7); "made nigh by the blood of Christ" (Eph. 2:13); "washed us from our sins in his own blood" (Rev. 1:5); "overcame him by the blood of the Lamb" (Rev. 12:11). Blood, the New Testament reveals, vividly symbolizes remission of sin, ransom, propitiation, justification, reconciliation, redemption, cleansing and victory. Men may talk glibly of "theories" of the atonement; the New Testament presents no theory but a uniform doctrine. And the shame of ecumenism in its present form is the avoidance of the biblical doctrine. It has refused to take on the offense of the blood.

That ecumenism struggles to ascertain the will of God in regard to the external structure of the church needs to be commended. That it does not yield to the authority of Scriptures in this search needs to be condemned. Christ has revealed the external structure of the church in New Testament Scripture. Each denomination must subject itself to the judgment of Scripture and on the day of judgment it will be manifest whether the structure be of gold, silver, precious stones, wood, hay, or stubble. Undoubtedly, the nearer we approach the heavenly pattern the less emphasis will there be on the external and earthly bonds that men hold so dear. One can be scattered and separated over the face of the earth, as were the Jews, yet show a solidarity that stems from the common worship of the living Temple.

THE FUTURE TEMPLE

"Beautiful for situation, the joy of the whole earth, is mount Zion," so spake the Psalmist concerning Zion upon which the holy Temple was built. That this is a figurative expression for the enlarged living Temple can be gleaned from the prophetic words of Malachi, "For from the rising of the sun even unto the going down of the same my name shall be great among the Gentiles; and in every place incense shall be offered unto my name and a pure offering: for my name shall be great among the heathen, saith the Lord of hosts." The New Testament, the infallible interpreter of Old Testament prophecy, applies the term temple to the church (1 Cor. 6:19; 2 Cor. 6:16; Eph. 2:19-22; 1 Pet. 2:5). The living Temple, which arose, as it were, out of the ashes of the old Temple, has had a glorious history and has been the joy of a multitude that no man can number.

Prophecy encourages us to look for a greater and more glorious Temple. Though it may be said from the rising of the sun even unto the going down of the same, incense is offered unto the name of our God, yet Zion is not the joy of *the whole earth* nor in every place is incense offered. True, many give an eschatological import to the glorious Old Testament prophecies, forgetting that the latter days for the prophets was the reign of the Messiah. Prophecy deals with time and history. Within time and history we may expect fulfilment by a great effusion of the Spirit. The church will again be instructed, "Enlarge the place of thy tent, and let them stretch forth the curtains of thine habitations: spare not, lengthen thy cords, and strengthen thy stakes; for thou shalt break forth on the right hand and on the left; and thy seed shall inherit the Gentiles, and make the desolate cities to be inhabited" (Isa. 54:2, 3). Jesus gave impetus to fulfilment of prophecy when he ordered the church, "Go ye therefore, and make disciples of all nations, baptizing them in the name of the Father, and of the Son, and of the Holy Ghost."

Recent ecumenical stress has been on the missionary program of the Church. The urgency to evangelize the world is pressed as a powerful incentive for churches to unite as one. But what is the evangel to be proclaimed to the heathen? What is the message of the missionary? Can there be united action without a common message? The great need of the ecumenical movement is to turn its face towards the holy Temple. The sole hope of unity among men and nations is the living Temple. The Temple is Christ—the crucified Christ. The greatest of all missionaries determined that he would know nothing save Jesus and him crucified. Christ and him crucified is the center of worship and unity. Wherever the crucified Christ is proclaimed incense shall be offered and a pure offering and the name of the Lord shall be great among the heathen. The living Temple will be enlarged to include a multitude which no man can number, of all nations, and kindreds, and people, and tongues.

Chapter XIII

THE COUNCILS

One indication of the ecumenical climate of the twentieth century is the formation of a number of councils and associations of churches. While the motivations for the establishment of these bodies are not entirely similar, an identical philosophy underlies them all. A council or association provides a cooperative agency to carry out matters of common interest and a vehicle to encourage fellowship among its member churches. Thus one discovers in the constitutions of these councils such statements as "inclusive cooperative agency"; "to represent the Evangelical Christians of America in matters calling for unity of action"; "an agency for fellowship and cooperation"; "dedication to a program of mutual helpfulness in the propagation of the Gospel, the defence of Christian liberties, and the attainment of objectives which are of common concern." All seem to feel the need of a cooperative agency and a common front for Christian action.

Not all denominations find representation in existing councils and associations. The Southern Baptist Convention, with a membership of over eight million, abstains from connection with any organization of churches. The Lutheran Missouri Synod and other Lutheran bodies, with over four million members, are outside of the fold of any national or international council. There are, of course, fellowships of denominations similar in doctrine and worship such as the Presbyterian Alliance and the Lutheran Federation of Churches. At present no organization exists that can claim to speak for the Protestant church as a whole.

EXISTING COUNCILS

At present three national councils exist in the United States with relationship in some degree to three world organizations. These organizations are:

> National Council of the Churches of Christ (NCC)
> World Council of Churches (WCC)
> National Association of Evangelicals (NAE)
> World Evangelical Fellowship (WEF)
> American Council of Christian Churches (ACCC)
> International Council of Christian Churches (ICCC)

The National Council of the Churches of Christ in the United States of America came into official existence on November 29, 1950, at a Constituting Convention in Cleveland, Ohio. The Council absorbed the following agencies of churches and combined their interests and functions:

> Federal Council of the Churches of Christ in America
> Foreign Missions Conference of North America
> Home Missions Council of North America
> International Council of Religious Education
> Missionary Education Movement of the United States and Canada
> National Protestant Council on Higher Education
> United Council of Church Women
> United Stewardship Council

The NCC claims to represent 30 church bodies with a grand total of 36,719,786 members. Regular meetings of the NCC General Assembly are convened triennially. The Council has a General Board that possesses full powers of the Council *ad interim*, except the power to determine the membership and power to revise its Constitution and Bylaws.

The World Council of Churches was organized at the World Assembly held in Amsterdam, Holland, in August, 1948. There are 165 constituent member Churches of the Council. The administrative responsibility is lodged in a Central Committee of ninety, elected by the Assembly which meets every sixth year.

The National Association of Evangelicals was officially organized in May, 1943, at Chicago, Illinois. The NAE claims to represent 40 denominations and a membership of one and three quarters million. The business of the Association is administered by a Board of Administration. The Association meets annually in the month of April or May.

The World Evangelical Fellowship came into organization August, 1951, at Woudschoten, Netherlands. Some 21 countries participated. The affairs of the Fellowship are managed by a General Committee, consisting of representatives from each constituent member. The Fellowship holds triennial international conferences.

The American Council of Christian Churches was organized in New York City, September 17, 1941. It represents 14 denominations and a general constituent membership of 230,368. Including those listed as adherents, the total membership claimed is 1,504,529. The Council meets at least once a year. The Executive Committee that conducts *ad interim* business consists of the officers, six members at large, and one member from each constituent member denomination.

The International Council of Christian Churches was formed in Amsterdam, The Netherlands, August, 1948. This Council consists of 57 constituent members from 23 countries. The Plenary Congress of the ICCC meets at least once in five years. The *ad interim* business of the Council is carried out by an Executive Committee.

STATEMENTS OF FAITH

By the very nature of representative Christian councils some statement of faith is required. A Christian council cannot be so inclusive as to include non-Christian organizations. For instance, the only way to eliminate Unitarian bodies is to define the person of Jesus Christ so as to manifest his deity. The National Council of Churches of Christ desired to be as latitudinarian as possible and therefore its statement of faith is reduced to a bare minimum. The NCC could not state less without losing any vestige of or resemblance to Christianity. One must glean the faith for which it stands in the very loose, indefinite and hazy Preamble of its Constitution, which reads as follows:

> In the Providence of God, the time has come when it seems fitting more fully to manifest oneness in Jesus Christ as Divine Lord and Saviour, by the creation of an inclusive co-operative agency of the Christian churches of the United States of America to continue and extend the following general agencies of the churches and to combine all their interests and functions: . . . .

One almost loses the affirmation of Jesus as Divine Lord and Saviour by its subordination to the main thought—to manifest oneness by the creation of an inclusive co-operative agency. One must not be deceived by the contention that the NCC is merely an agency. This "agency" has taken upon itself the direction of Christian education, life, and work. It has entered into the area and sphere of the Church and therefore must give some idea of its confession. It cannot direct, guide and instruct without formulating its message. In the present theological climate the assertion of "Jesus Christ as Divine Lord and Saviour" is meaningless as diverse interpretations exist within the framework of the NCC.

The World Council of Churches adopted a more direct and meaningful statement of faith. Not without opposition from those who felt that the meager sentence was too narrow and exclusive, the WCC adopted the following as its basis:

> The World Council of Churches is a fellowship of Churches which accept our Lord Jesus Christ as God and Saviour.

While this basis is good as far as it goes, the statement is entirely too inadequate for the situation in which the WCC finds itself. There seems to be a tacit agreement that one may interpret the statement at will. That this is done is revealed by Professor John Knox, "Objection has often been raised to this formula; as we have seen, it is not a characteristically biblical statement, and, moreover, it is theologically inadequate, since it ignores the humanity of Jesus. Furthermore, it appears to have been adopted originally without much deliberation, indeed almost by accident. But the later refusal to alter it in response to criticism illustrates the truth (which I believe the whole history of Christology will demonstrate) that where a greater or lesser name is proposed for Christ, it is always the greater that is adopted. And this is true, I repeat, because the name of the person is really a symbol of the significance of the event; and the church finds it impossible to minimize that significance" (*The Early Church*, p. 80). To Dr. Knox the allegation that Jesus is God is nothing more than a mere symbol. If the World Council of Churches does not accept his interpretation, it must so define the person of Christ that one may know the significance of the formula. The WCC must have the same courage and perseverance of the ancient ecumenical councils which clearly define the person of Christ against all heresy. It must without fear face the cost of confessing the historic Christian faith.

Only the National Association of Evangelicals and the American Council of Christian Churches recognize in their statements of faith that Christianity is a revealed religion and has an authoritative source of revelation. Of the two Confessions the ACCC statement is more carefully drawn up. Regarding authority the ACCC believes:

> The plenary divine inspiration of the Scriptures in the original languages, their consequent inerrancy and infallibility, and, as the Word of God, the supreme and final authority in faith and life.

Actually no good reason exists why the National Council and the World Council cannot include a statement on the authority of Scripture in faith and life. Both have made dogmatic statements concerning the person of Jesus and one may ask, from whence have they obtained this knowledge? They must acknowledge that the titles of Jesus (Saviour, Lord, God) find their source in Scripture. Much of the deliberation of the NCC and WCC has been done in the atmosphere of dying liberalism. Liberalism contended that the Creator of language could not communicate accurate thought to his creatures. Surely it is time to exchange the liberal concept of an impotent and helpless God for the catholic and evangelical concept of the omnipotent God. Sooner or later authority of Scripture must be defined.

The doctrinal statements of the NAE and the ACCC include

more than the authority of Scripture. They affirm the Trinity. They affirm the essential, absolute, eternal deity, and real and proper, but sinless, humanity of Jesus. In so doing they keep continuity with catholic faith of many centuries. The virgin birth, substitutionary atonement, bodily resurrection and second coming are also affirmed. Concerning soteriology, these doctrines are declared: the depravity of man, justification by faith, regeneration by the Holy Spirit, eternal life and death. The real spiritual unity of the redeemed in Christ is also asserted. These doctrines are not the property of "fundamentalists" but belong to the creeds of historic denominations. They are sufficiently narrow to weed out those who are out of sympathy with the historic Christian faith and sufficiently broad to include the great majority of denominations that adhere to their confessions.

The American Council of Christian Churches, however, has an additional condition for membership: no national church or association which is a member of the National Council of Churches is eligible for constituent membership. In the Preamble judgment is made that many professing churches and whole denominations are apostate. The charge is also made of autocratic domination on the part of modernistic leaders. On the other hand, the National Association of Evangelicals welcomes all those who are prepared to accept and comply with its doctrinal statement. Needless to say the two organizations do not look kindly at each other and thus give the impression that evangelicals are sorely divided.

Large evangelical bodies such as the Missouri Synod of the Lutheran Church and the Southern Baptists have remained out of the evangelical national councils and their world counterparts. Also many evangelicals have membership in denominations connected with the National Council of Churches. One cannot obtain a fair picture either of the number of evangelicals or their strength by limiting appraisal to the NAE and ACCC. Within many denominations there is a resurgence of the traditional evangelism and this revival will undoubtedly reveal its power in the near future.

NOT A SUPER-CHURCH

Fears have been expressed frequently that the existing Councils may take on the nature of a Super-Church. Such a charge has been levelled at the World Council of Churches. To answer this charge the Central Committee of the Council, meeting at Toronto, Ontario, 1950, prepared a document entitled, *The Church, the Churches, and the World Council of Churches*. It calls attention to a resolution adopted at the first Assembly at Amsterdam which reads, in part, "But the Council is far from desiring to usurp any of the functions which already belong to its constituent churches, or to control them, or to legislate for them, and indeed is prevented by its constitution from doing so. Moreover, while earnestly seeking fellowship in thought and action for all its members, the Council disavows any thought of becoming a single unified church structure independent of the churches which have joined in constituting the Council, or a structure dominated by a centralized administrative authority." That this resolution did not allay fears is seen in the need for further statement.

In the "further statement" of the Toronto document, page 5, the assertion is made, "The World Council deals in a provisional way with divisions between existing churches, which ought not to be, because they contradict the very nature of the Church." Thus the Council passes judgment on the churches it represents and assumes that every division ought not to be because it contradicts the very nature of the Church. The World Council does have a definite conception of the nature of the Church—sufficient to condemn denominationalism as contradicting the very nature of the Church—in spite of its protest on page 7, "The World Council cannot and should not be based on any one particular conception of the Church. It does not prejudge the ecclesiological problem." If concluding that existing divisions contradict the very nature of the Church is not prejudging the ecclesiological problem, we do not know what could be.

However, the Toronto document affirms on page 6, *The World Council of Churches is not and must never become a Super-Church*. This strong disavowal does not satisfy the Congregationalist, Dr. Marion J. Bradshaw, who writes, "The most interesting question in this discussion among the Congregationalists arises from the fact that the General Council of Congregational Christian Churches claims to have acquired, without necessity of approval or right of hindrance by the churches, the right and power to turn the fellowship of free churches into a national unitary or corporate church. The significance of this controversy is heightened by the fact that the World Council of Churches is now saying to member churches substantially what was stated and promised to the free churches when the National Council of Congregational Churches was formed in 1865-1871" (*Free Churches and Christian Unity*, p. 13).

The above apprehension is not put at rest by the suggestion of Dr. Charles Morrison that ecumenical leaders feel that it would be tactically unwise to define sharply the goal of the Councils lest it alienate some denominations. He writes, "Naturally, therefore, those who guide the movement hesitate frankly to suggest that its goal would necessarily involve some adjustment, if not radical abandonment, of the denominational system" (*The Unfinished Reformation*, p. 49). Nor is this fear put at rest by the statement of Bishop Newbigin, ". . . there is a real danger of our forgetting that the World Council only has a right to exist as a means to something further, as a stage on the way from disunity to unity; and that if it comes to be regarded as itself the proper form of the Church's unity in Christ, it will become committed to a disastrous error. I believe that membership in the World Council is indeed the way that God has opened up in our time by which the Churches may move from disunity to unity, and that to refuse this way would be to refuse God's call. But it is the way, not the end, and if it comes to be regarded as the end it must be condemned as the wrong end" (*The Household of God*, p. 15). Dr. Peter Brunner, Professor of Systematic Theology at the University of Heidelberg, Germany, catches the same sound. He writes, "There are many signs which indicate that the work of the World Council of Churches has reached a decisive stage. Church bodies are therein joined together through official delegations. The registered tables of agreements and disagreements among these churches may be said now to have been completed. There is also widespread agreement that the churches dare not be satisfied merely with brotherly co-operation in facing practical tasks, valuable as that may be. The sentiment is now expressed: 'We must move forward! We dare not lose sight of the goal of the ecumenical movement! This goal is the full union of our divided churches. We must now travel new roads which will bring us closer to this goal!' " (*The Unity of the Church, A Symposium*, p. 11).

The views expressed in the above quotations are not the official pronouncements of the World Council but do come from those within the Council. It is no hidden fact that many hope that the World Council will be the instrument to create a single unified church structure even though the Council itself may never be that structure. Its expressed view that present divisions contradict the very nature of the Church, compells it to work diligently for the eradication of denominations.

The National Council of Churches of Christ makes the same disavowal of any intention to be a Super-Church. In a leaflet titled, *The National Council of Churches, What Is It*, the question is asked, "What authority has the Council over the Churches?" The answer given is, "None. It is in no sense a superchurch or superorganization. It depends wholly on the principle of voluntary co-operation through democratic representative processes. It is completely committed to the maintenance of our cherished freedom. It rejects all thought of enforced uniformity. It seeks only the kind of unity which is consistent with liberty and diversity. . . . Co-operation does not require any church to relinquish any part of its own historic heritage. The Council can, therefore, have a great Christian influence without exercising any control over any church." The Constitution affirms, "The Council shall have no authority or administrative control over the churches which constitute its membership. It shall have no authority to prescribe a common creed, or form of church government, or form of worship, or to limit the autonomy of the churches co-operating in it."

Serious consideration should be given to changing the name of the National Council *of* Churches to National Council *for* Churches to conform to its evident character and function. The General Board, which accomplishes the real work of the Council through its divisions and committees, had a voting constituency of 169 at the September, 1957, meeting in New York. Only 91 (54%) directly represented denominations. A resolution was prepared for the General Assembly of 1957 that has the practical effect of further decreasing denominational representation by enlarging representation from state, city and local councils. Even within the Board it was pointed out that if this resolution is adopted the direction will be further and further away from being a Council *of* Churches.

The direction of counsel does not flow from the Churches to the National Council but the very opposite. The National Council floods the Churches with statements on missions, worship, evangelism, economics, religious education, social and moral responsibilities, community projects and so forth. Some of their statements are to be commended and show evidence of genuine research. Others are of questionable value and may have a baneful influence. For instance, taking over the functions of the Foreign Missions Conference of North America has not helped the cause of missions. The proportion of missionaries under the Division of Foreign Missions of the Council is sharply decreasing (cf Chapter I) and churches may well reconsider the wisdom of associating with the Council in missionary endeavors.

The Constitution of the National Council states that it shall have no authority to prescribe a common creed. Nevertheless, teachings opposing tenets of member Churches appear in a booklet recommended for study by the Churches. The title of this booklet is *The Good News of God* and the subtitle, *The Nature and Task of Evangelism.* In this booklet the doctrine of total depravity is rejected, "There is no need to assert again the extravagances that led great numbers of Christians to reject the doctrine—no need to assert man's fall from original perfection into total depravity, or a physical inheritance of guilt by children yet unborn." This is hard to square with the assertion of the Westminster Confession of Faith, "By this sin they (Adam and Eve) fell from their original righteousness and communion with God, and so became dead in sin, and wholly defiled in all the faculties and parts of soul and body. They being the root of all mankind, the guilt of this sin was imputed, and the same death in sin and corrupted nature conveyed to all their posterity, descending from them by ordinary generation." Nor does it square with Ephesians 2:3, "And were by nature the children of wrath, even as others" and Romans 5:12, "Wherefore, as by one man sin entered into the world, and death by sin; and so death passed upon all men, for that all have sinned." Paul's whole argument of the imputation of Christ's righteousness falls to the ground if the imputation of Adam's guilt is not true, as asserted by the Council's booklet. When the Council presumes to formulate theology let the churches beware.

The problem of taking over the function of the church also troubled the National Association of Evangelicals. First its policy was to employ evangelists to conduct campaigns under its auspices. This dismayed some members who differed on the method and content of evangelism. In 1950 the NAE decided to assist in the promotion of evangelism but to leave the actual functioning of evangelism to the churches themselves. The member churches guarded the proper function of the Church— the teaching and preaching of the Gospel of Jesus Christ.

There will be constant temptation to the various Councils to take over the proper functions of the Church. Because of refusal to grapple with the problems of the day and a willingness to take the path of least resistance, some churches may yield to the pressure of the Councils and surrender their proper functions. There will be a constant temptation for a Council to proclaim itself as the voice of the church without receiving the message from the constituent churches. When Councils become more than agencies for co-operative work and enter into the functions of the Church, then they take on the nature of a Super-Church despite disavowals. Against this the churches must constantly be on guard.

Chapter XIV.

EVANGELICAL DISUNITY

No choicer segment of the visible church exists that can bring to realization the true ecumenical goal than the group known as evangelicals in the biblical and historical sense of that much abused word. Evangelicals have the same infallible rule for faith and life: they believe the Scriptures to be the objective revelation of God; they are in fundamental agreement as to the means by which they can grow in the knowledge of the written revelation. Their numerical strength is greater than appears on the surface and is not limited to known conservative denominations; they are to be found in almost all churches. Many are not articulate but carry an effective witness without trumpet and fanfare. Some are just becoming aroused with the realization of the current drift away from evangelical Christianity. Their number is such that they can do much to actualize the unity of the faith unto the measure of the stature of the fulness of Christ—the goal of biblical ecumenism.

But, alas, no segment within the visible church has greater reputation for disunity than the evangelicals. This questionable distinction is in a measure earned and in a measure, unearned.

REPUTATION DESERVED

History does reveal that at times evangelical denominations, although in agreement on the vital doctrines of the Christian faith, have viewed each other as rival kingdoms struggling for the souls of men. A bitter and partisan spirit refused to acknowledge that they were brothers in Christ. Each, on occasion, have sought the ruin of the other on the pretext of serving the Lord. In controversy, men have been fierce, implacable, and revengeful. That they became so because of the impulsion to defend what they considered vital truth does not excuse their treading down with hatred those who trusted in the same Lord for salvation. In their bitter zeal they were persecuting those whom the Lord loved. Their contention for the faith is not to be condemned but rather the bitterness and absence of Christian charity with which they conducted controversy. And it must be acknowledged that part of the drive to eliminate denominationalism has sprung from the unsavory history connected with it.

Having said the above and having acknowledged the truth of it, one must state in fairness that in this fault the evangelical does not stand alone. The myth has been exploded that liberals and modernists are always loving and tolerant. The viciousness with which some have attacked those who hold the traditional fundamentals of the Gospel is too well known to need further comment. They are tolerant of every heresy except the "heresy" of orthodoxy. The presence of modernists within the denominations is ample evidence that evangelicals have been actually too tolerant.

Appalled at the growth of unbelief within the historic denominations, evangelical groups have broken away to form independent congregations. This has given evidence to the charge that evangelicals are divisive and have no concern for the unity of the church. There are groups of Christians who have not seriously considered the sin of schism, who have lost sight of the nature of the church and who have not had the fortitude to battle for the faith within the denomination. Not infrequently they have been the most vociferous among the evangelicals and have received publicity far beyond their relative size. We do not refer to those who have been forced out of denominations because of loyalty to Christ and his Word, but to those who seem to be separatist by nature and devoid of proper concern for the church at large.

History also reveals that divisions have been caused by differences on non-essentials or on the basis of human leadership. For instance, at the present time serious splits are being caused by divergent views of the pretribulation and post-tribulation rapture of the church in connection with the second coming of the Lord. Since error breeds error, one should not question the right and the duty of Christians to warn against the least variation or turning aside from the teaching of the Word. But where the difference hinges on a particular interpretation that does not hazard the vital doctrines of the faith one must not allow the heat engendered by controversy to flare into separation and division. Where the creedal statements of the denomination are not involved separation becomes schism. Also Christians should beware of following human leaders, even though they be outstanding evangelicals, whose individualism causes them to leave a denomination. Such have contributed to the conviction that evangelicals are by nature separatists and advocates of disunity.

REPUTATION UNDESERVED

Fairness should reject the imputation of divisiveness upon all evangelicals because of a relatively small group who recklessly run into schism and who seem motivated by a desire for publicity and a spirit of belligerency. If issues are not forthcoming, they manufacture them. Their support comes from those who are impressed by noise and shouting. There are many sores—grievous sores—on the body ecclesia. They attract a certain type of evangelical as physical sores attract flies. They buzz and molest but make no real attempt to apply the balm of Gilead or the surgical sword of the Spirit. They gloat over sores and shed no tears. They cater to the appetite of sensationalism. They even castigate fellow evangelicals for not following in their ways and using their methods. Fairminded people will not allow such antics to color their impression of evangelicals.

Sometimes evangelicals are looked upon as propagators of disunity because of refusal to take part in current movements that involve disloyal compromise. They oppose certain popular trends because of their loyalty to denominational creeds, to Scriptures, and to their Lord. They have been called reactionaries and divisive because they refuse to follow that leadership they judge to be destructive of Christian faith. The opposition does not come from a native stubbornness but faithfulness to vows given before God and men. They are not willing to sell their birthright for a mess of pottage. Often heartache, loneliness and frustration are their lot. It would be far easier to drift with the ecclesiastical current. But they place truth before peace even as Scripture, "The wisdom which is from above is *first* pure, *then* peaceable." They resist every attempt to reconcile differences among Christians that involve the sacrifice of truth. They believe that neither Christianity nor the church can survive the destruction of vital truths. Indeed they are fighters; they are contenders for the faith which was once delivered unto the saints. But this does not make them purveyors of disunity. When the smoke of battle is cleared in the passing of time their position will be seen as that which strengthened the bulwarks of the church against the adversary. Even at this present time many grant the strength and wisdom of evangelicalism and are embracing some of its tenets. They have left some of the husks of liberalism and are groping towards historic Christianity. Evangelicals, by the maintenance of scriptural truth, have contributed more to the real unity of the church than those who yielded so easily to the wiles of a liberalism that has weakened the church and prepared it for secular invasion.

Large and small evangelical denominations have remained out of the National Council of Churches and as a result have been accused of being disinterested in the cause of church unity and co-operation. Since the National Council is not a Super-Church and does not claim to be the *Una Sancta*, refusal to become a member does not evidence a disinclination to work for the cause of church unity. Certain pronouncements and propaganda of the National Council have caused denominations to wonder whether membership in the Council may not undermine their evangelical position and destroy their traditional freedom to propagate the Gospel wherever they are led and by what means they choose. They look with dismay at the attempt to control radio religious broadcasting and the attempt of local councils to dictate the establishment of new churches. Their refusal to jeopardize their heritage of doctrine and freedom should not be interpreted as disinterest in the cause of true unity. When men differ on important questions of faith and action, it is far better to maintain freedom of belief and life, than to pretend to agree or to become discordant elements in an uncongenial union.

FUTURE UNITY

The very existence of denominations gives evidence of disunity. Churches are in disagreement on questions of polity, sacraments, worship, and theology. Three general systems of polity prevail: episcopal, presbyterian and congregational. In the ecumenical movement Episcopalians have proved most adamant in regard to their position on church government and orders. Indeed, some ecumenists suggest that the only way to bring about a united church is to accept the historic episcopate and that all nonconformist ministers be ordained by an Episcopalian bishop. Realization has also come to the ecumenical movement that the sacraments, which are the visible signs of Christian unity, form a strong and almost immovable obstacle in the achievement of the ecumenical goal. Lutheran and Reformed Churches are at variance on the doctrine of the Lord's Supper. The position of believer's baptism versus infant baptism is also a serious hindrance. In theology, the nature of the Church has been of foremost importance because it deals in a practical way with the achievement of the ecumenical goal. The study of this subject has shown a variety of views. As a rule the ecumenical movement prefers to leave theology in a dormant condition. However, the resurgence of Confessionalism will bring theology to the forefront and place further obstacles in the establishment of a single church structure.

The mood and nature of contemporary ecumenism make for a very poor instrument to achieve unity, especially as defined in Scripture. We would define biblical ecumenism as the movement in the universal visible church upon earth by which, under the influence and guidance of the Holy Spirit, the church comes into the unity of the faith and of the knowledge of the Son of God unto the measure of the stature of the fulness of Christ. True, an external structure can be formed by ecclesiastical pressures, by negligence of doctrine, by refusal of men to think for themselves—but is that the unity for which Christ prayed and will it result in permanent unity? Ecumenism will never in a thousand and one years achieve the goal of Christian unity until it settles the question of authority. Has God revealed the way, the truth, and the life for ecumenism in the written Word or is changing human experience authoritative? Is Christianity the revealed religion? Sooner or later ecumenism must grapple with the question of authority even as it is struggling with the doctrine of the nature of the church. As long as everyone has an authority, a confession, a Lord, a Christ, a church, we despair of the realization of unity.

Evangelicals have settled the question of authority. They build their faith, their creeds, their churches upon the foundation of the apostles and prophets, Christ Jesus himself being the chief corner stone. They strive to be apostolic in doctrine. They subordinate human creeds to Scriptures. While it is true that some regard their particular creeds as thoroughly agreeable to Scripture, nevertheless, they maintain the principle that the inscripturated Word is the final authority for faith and life and that human creeds must constantly be judged by Scriptures. It is because evangelicals have found the common source for their creeds in the Bible that they can say with sincerity and truth that their agreements are far greater than their disagreements. On vital doctrines they do not have "to agree to disagree." The creeds of historic denominations show wonderful accord on the authority of Scripture, Trinity, creation, fall of man, deity of Christ, justification, saving faith, the last judgment, heaven and hell, and the second coming of the Lord.

Since evangelicals have come far to conformity of doctrine because of a common norm, the prospect of greater harmony is always possible. Most of their energy in the first part of the twentieth century has been consumed in the battle against those who would destroy the basic structure of Christianity. With Israel of old they can complain, "O God, the heathen are come into thine inheritance; thy holy temple have they defiled; they have laid Jerusalem on heaps" (Ps. 79:1). Heathen, indeed, have taken over their halls of learning and robbed them of their heritage. And Liberalism must be held responsible, to a great extent, for holding up the cause of unity by leading the church into a dead-end street. It is devoutly to be hoped that the church may be given a period of rest in which she can meditate on the law and the prophets and perform constructive work in the areas where disagreements still exist. Evangelicals have made little advance in theological studies during the past half century, partly due to the necessity of vindicating Christian doctrine and exposing heresy. The prospect for immediate rest from this labor is rather dim as heresy has changed her scarlet garment for one less obvious which blends more into the coloring of historic Christianity. However, the resurgence of Confessionalism under the influence and guidance of the Holy Spirit may lead the church into the more constructive paths. Under no circumstances can vigilance against heresy be relaxed. But regardless of circumstances evangelicals must enter more deeply into the study of the Word.

For greater strength and unity, the areas of differences must be investigated in the light of Scripture. As long as differences remain denominations must be willing to enter into conversation with those who differ from them. The World Council of Churches must be commended for assembling representatives of churches to discuss the nature of the unity we need. This sets an example for evangelicals to do likewise. The increase of independent congregations and ecumenism brings this question to the foreground. Little work has been done in recent years by conservatives on this subject while dozens of books have been written by ecumenists. Orthodox Christians have been slothful and neglectful, yielding the field to those who do not hold to the full authority of the written Word. While evangelicals do not consider the question of church government a major concern of the church, nevertheless, it is of great importance. Christ has given revelation concerning it in the New Testament and if the church is not functioning according to the direction of the Head of the church, great harm can result.

Another area for discussion is the doctrine of baptism. The doctrine of baptism has been brought to life recently by Karl Barth's position on infant baptism. The discussion, however, has been limited to Europe. Naturally the subject is delicate and will stir up controversy. The doctrine involves more than the mode of baptism; it touches on the whole question of the covenant. Pierre Ch. Marcel writes, "The celebrated dogmatician H. Bavinck has well remarked that the doctrine of the sacraments has always been the shibboleth, the touchstone, of every dogmatic system. It is there that the principles from which one sets off in the Church and theology, in questions of faith and of life, find their practical and concrete issue. The doctrines of the affinities of God and the world, of creation and regeneration, of Christ's divine and human natures, of the modes of action of the Holy Spirit, of sin and of grace, of spirit and of matter, are all more or less present and implicit in the doctrine of the sacraments. The diverse roads of theology converge, whether one wishes it or not, sooner or later, consciously or unconsciously, in the highway of the sacraments" (*The Biblical Doctrine of Infant Baptism,* p. 17). This doctrine also has important implications for the ecumenical movement as some teach that by the act of water baptism one is incorporated into the body of Christ. As the church engages into the study of the sacrament of baptism, she will learn that more than a few proof texts are involved. For the sake of closer unity, however, the church must engage in viewing this doctrine in the light of Scripture.

The same need for diligent study applies to the sacrament of the Lord's Supper. The ecumenical movement has become painfully aware that the Lord's Supper instead of revealing the unity of Church actually points up the divisions that exist in the visible church. At ecumenical gatherings three or four communion services must be held as all cannot, on principle, sit at the same table. To some ecumenists life in the body of Christ is sustained by participation in the Lord's Supper. Grace flows to the believer through this sacrament. The question of Christ's presence in the sacrament has divided the Lutherans and the Reformed. Both are adamant in their views and feel that the last word has been spoken. Here and there a lone Lutheran or Reformed voice can be heard suggesting that both positions seek again the judgment of Scripture. Not for the purpose of organizational unity, but for greater spiritual unity, conversation should be engaged between those holding divergent views.

Today little is heard among church members in regard to Arminianism and Calvinism. We suspect that this has stemmed from the neglect of the Scriptures and indifference to the question of salvation. Ignorance of this subject is not restricted to the laity. Historically this question has divided Methodist and Reformed bodies. With the resurgence of Bible study Christians will again delve into the questions of election and grace. Neo-orthodoxy has stirred up discussion on these doctrines among the theologians. Since teachings on election and grace have caused serious divisions in the past, the church, by diligent study, should discover what revelation has to say and thus spare the future church from bitter divisions.

Some evangelicals are concerned chiefly about the doctrine of eschatology. Sometimes the questions that surround the second coming of the Lord have consumed their time and energy to such a degree that they have neglected other vital doctrines. There are three schools of thought concerning the doctrine of the last thing: premillennialism, amillennialism, and postmillennialism. All agree on the second visible return of the Lord. The pre-millennialists teach that the millennium will be inaugurated upon earth with the Lord's return. The other two schools of thought teach that the Lord's return will terminate history and inaugurate the kingdom of glory.

All three schools of thought have demonstrated that they can live more or less happily in one denomination. The question, however, has caused some division and has led to the establishment of independent churches. Some would minimize the importance of determining the scriptural truth concerning eschatology as long as there is agreement on the visible return of the Lord. However, we are convinced that these matters are of utmost importance to the church. They have bearing on the nature of the church and the future of the church. Those who feel that the church is doomed and that her rapture into heaven will soon take place will react differently from those who expect a glorious future on earth for the church. The whole system of interpretation of Scripture is vitally involved. Without seeking to judge which school of thought is in error, it must be pointed out that it is a serious question. Since it occupies the center of interest to many, the various schools of thought must enter into conversation with each other without bitterness and rancor. Under the providence of God certain doctrines take prominence at certain periods of history. The doctrine of eschatology has this prominence in the present generation. Should not the church, then, determine to search the Scriptures and formulate the doctrine? The Word of God must be the only test and touchstone to try the teachings of men. This will take patience, forbearance, and love.

Other doctrines divide evangelical Christians. However, there is a wonderful agreement in the principal articles of the Christian faith. Mutual love would give visibility to this agreement and would be one of the quickest and best ways of convincing the world of the truth of the traditional fundamentals of the Christian faith. The world has some ground for believing that greater love exists among liberals and modernists than among evangelicals. In the midst of differences of interpretation of the infallible Word, love should be manifest, prayer should be engaged in one for another, imputing evil motives should be discarded, condemning a brother should be unknown, patience should be exercised, and humbleness in receiving light from others should be displayed.

In spite of weaknesses and imperfections, no choicer group exists to bring the true ecumenical goal than those who yield to the authority of the Word, acknowledge the true deity of the Lord, believe in the vicarious atonement, and wait for the coming of the Lord.

Chapter XV

THE COMING GREAT CHURCH

The Coming Great Church has been the theme of ecumenism and the dream of ecumenists. To some the dream will be realized when all Christians—Protestant, Orthodox, and Roman Catholic—will be in one corporate structure. The drive of ecumenism is to achieve this goal. Unity of faith, of worship, of doctrine must be subordinated to unity of polity. When all Christian people are shepherded under one organization the ecumenical millennium will have arrived.

Evangelicals are divided concerning the future of the Church. The premillennialist has no hope of any future glory for the Church and looks only for her rapture either before or after the great tribulation in connection with the second coming of Christ. The future glory of the earth is the establishment of the Jewish Kingdom over which Christ will reign a thousand years in Jerusalem. The visible church, to them, will take on an increasing apostate nature as the coming of the Lord draws near. A growing school of thought, amillennialist, holds that there is no sufficient scriptural ground for the expectation of a future golden age for the church and relates much of biblical prophecy to the intermediate state in heaven or the Kingdom of God in its consummate and eternal form. A third school of thought, postmillennialist, flourished under the influence of Jonathan Edwards, the Princeton theologians Charles and A. A. Hodge, J. A. Alexander, B. B. Warfield and the famous Southern Presbyterian theologians, J. H. Thornwell and R. L. Dabney. The evangelical postmillennialist looks for a fulfillment of the Old Testament prophecies of a glorious age of the Church upon earth through the preaching of the true Gospel under the power of the Holy Spirit. This school, long dormant, shows evidence of new life.

The writer belongs to the school that looks for a more glorious future for the church in time and history before the second coming of the Lord. Prophecy concerns itself with time and history and not with the consummate kingdom in its eternal form except for incidental reference. Many wonder how in a time of great distress, of flagrant sin, of secularism and unbelief within the church, how one can ever believe in the Coming Great Church. Isaiah lived in a time when Israel was apostate yet looked forward to the glorious days of the Messiah. The future should be determined not by contemporary events but from the Word of God. Many at this time are reading the pages of history to determine the future; far better that they read the book of the Lord of history.

Does the Bible teach that the Church of Christ will be established throughout the earth, that all nations will in time be predominantly Christ's, that the kingdom of Satan will be destroyed, and that there will be a universal prevalence of truth and peace throughout the earth? Does the Bible teach that this will be brought about by the preaching of the gospel along with the supernatural influence of the Holy Spirit? From Genesis to Revelation that is the encouragement of the written Word.

THE PROTEVANGELIUM

The triumph of the Church in history and upon the earth is first clearly indicated in Genesis 3:15, "And I will put enmity between thee and the woman, and between thy seed and her seed; it shall bruise thy head, and thou shalt bruise his heel." That this is indicative of the triumph of the Church upon earth is the interpretation of the prophets, the apostles and our Lord.

Genesis 3:15 is part of the curse pronounced against the serpent that commenced with verse 14 which contains the expression, "and dust shalt thou eat all the days of thy life." This becomes a figurative expression for victory throughout the Bible.

Psalm 72:8 prophesies concerning the Messiah, "He shall have dominion also from sea to sea, and from the river unto the ends of the earth." This is followed by the expression, "and his enemies shall lick the dust." In Micah 7:17 we read of the defeat of the enemies of the Church, "They shall lick the dust like a serpent." Isaiah 49:23 prophesies of the future Church, "And kings shall be thy nursing fathers, and their queens thy nursing mothers: they shall bow down to thee with their face toward the earth, and lick up the dust of thy feet." In the glorious millennial blessings promised in Isaiah 65 we read in verse 25, "The wolf and the lamb shall feed together, and the lion shall eat straw like the bullock: and dust shall be the serpent's meat."

In the New Testament reference to the victory promised in Genesis is found in Luke 10 where the Lord said this after hearing of the successful preaching mission of the seventy, "I beheld Satan as lightning fall from heaven. Behold, I give unto you power to tread on serpents and scorpions, and over all the power of the enemy: and nothing shall by any means hurt you." This figurative expression reveals that through the preaching of the Gospel Satan was cast from his high heaven to the dust of the earth. Through preaching the gospel the disciples tread upon the Serpent. Satan was to receive a crushing blow not through a cataclysmic act at the second coming but by the preaching of the gospel. Paul relates the same truth in Romans 16:20, "And the God of peace shall bruise Satan under your feet shortly." Not by a cataclysmic act, but by the feet of Christians Satan was to be crushed in the Roman Empire. The decisive defeat of Satan by the gospel is seen in Revelation 12:9, 11, "And the great dragon was cast out, that old serpent, called the Devil, and Satan which deceiveth the whole world: he was cast out into the earth, and his angels were cast out with him. . . . And they overcame him by the blood of the Lamb, and by the word of their testimony." Not by a cataclysmic act, but by the blood of the Lamb.

ALL NATIONS BLESSED

Another great promise referred to throughout Scripture is that of the Abrahamic covenant, "and in thee shall all families of the earth be blessed" (Gen. 12:3; 17:5, 6; 22:18; 28:14, etc.).

Paul interprets this to mean that the seed of Abraham will inherit the world, "For the promise, that he should be the heir of the world, was not to Abraham, or to his seed, through the law, but through the righteousness of faith" (Rom. 4:13). To this, surely, we can relate the promise of Christ in the Sermon on the Mount, "Blessed are the meek: for they shall inherit the earth." Also related to the covenant promise is the Great Commission, "Go therefore, and make disciples of all nations" (ASV). God is a covenant-keeping God and Christ commands the church to fulfill the covenant. We do not honor God by reducing the covenant concept of "all nations blessed" to a bare representation of all nations. We, under the grace and power of Christ, are to make disciples of all nations.

In Genesis 13 where the covenant promise is repeated to Abraham after his separation from Lot, God states this: "Lift up now thine eyes, and look from the place where thou art northward, and southward, and eastward, and westward: for all the land which thou seest, to thee will I give it, and to thy seed forever. And I will make thy seed as the dust of the earth: so that if a man can number the dust of the earth, then shall thy seed also be numbered." In looking toward four directions Abraham could look but for a few miles. In reality his vision took in the entire world as Paul reveals in Romans 4:13. But notice how this expression, "north, south, east, and west," comes up throughout the Bible. In Genesis 28:14 it is repeated to Jacob: "And thy seed shall be as the dust of the earth, and thou shalt spread abroad to the west, and to the east, and to the north, and to the south: and in thee and in thy seed shall all the families of the earth be blessed." Moses relates in Deuteronomy 3:27 how the promise was repeated to him, "Get thee up into the top of Pisgah, and lift up thine eyes westward, and northward, and southward, and eastward, and behold it with thine eyes." In the Tabernacle the porters were to be at the gates, "In four quarters were the porters, toward the east, west, north, and south" (1 Chron. 9:24). And the molten sea was supported by twelve oxen who looked towards the north, west, south, and the east; thus typifying that the cleansing signified by the molten sea was for the entire world.

The prophets also carry the thought of these directions as indicated in Psalm 107:3 and Isaiah 43:5. Our Lord indicated that his rejection by the Jews would not frustrate this promise of God as he related in Luke 13:28, 29: "There shall be weeping and gnashing of teeth, when ye shall see Abraham, and Isaac, and Jacob, and all the prophets, in the kingdom of God, and you yourselves thrust out. And they shall come from the east, and from the west, and from the north, and from the south, and shall sit down in the kingdom of God." Here our Lord includes the Gentiles in the covenant. The apostle John gathers in that aspect also in his vision of the Lamb's Bride, the Holy City. In Revelation 21:13 we read, "On the east three gates; on the north three gates; on the south three gates; and on the west three gates." And these gates are open to the entire world as is stated in verse 25.

The blessings offered in the Covenant made with Abraham are ours. A vital part of that covenant is the promise that the Church would be a blessing to all nations. Already we have seen that fulfilled in part. It should require but little faith on our part to believe in a greater fulfillment of the covenant. It should fill our hearts with hope and thankfulness that through Christ and His Church all nations without exception will be blessed.

MESSAGE OF PSALMS

The Covenant concept of "all nations blessed" comes to the fore in the poetry of the Psalter. The composers of the Book of Praise of the Old Testament looked for the triumph of the Church upon earth. They rejoiced in this concept for it would redound to the glory of their God. There are no better missionary hymns than those contained in the Psalms. One of the contributing factors to the present day pessimism, gloominess, defeatism, within the Church is the omitting of the Psalms from the hymn books. They should have first place. The best musical talent of the Church should be occupied in setting the Psalms to fitting music.

In the beginning of the Psalter we are introduced to the fact of the triumph of the Messiah. In Psalm 2:8 is the statement: "Ask of me, and I shall give thee the heathen for thine inheritance, and the uttermost parts of the earth for thy possession."

That Christ did ask for the heathen as an inheritance and the uttermost parts of the earth for his possession is seen in the Great Commission. In Matthew it states: "Make disciples of all nations"; in Mark: "Go into all the world, and preach the gospel to every creature"; in Luke: "And that repentance and remission of sins should be preached in his name among all nations"; and in Acts: "Ye shall be witnesses unto me both in Jerusalem, and in all Judea, and in Samaria, and unto the uttermost part of the earth." The latter expression is borrowed from the second Psalm.

In Psalm 22, after a description of the crucifixion of the Messiah, the note of triumph is given in verses 27 and 28, "All the ends of the world shall remember and turn unto the Lord: and all the kindreds of the nations shall worship before thee. For the kingdom is the Lord's: and he is the governor among the nations." This not only shows that the world will turn to the Lord but that it will be the result of his crucifixion as is also clearly revealed in Isaiah.

Psalm 72 is the classic of the universal triumph of Christ. Here are a few verses: "In his days shall the righteous flourish; and abundance of peace so long as the moon endureth. He shall have dominion also from sea to sea, and from the river unto the ends of the earth. . . . The kings of Tarshish and of the isles shall bring presents: the kings of Sheba and Seba shall offer gifts. Yea, all kings shall fall down before him: all nations shall serve him. . . . All nations shall call him blessed." Here are a few more samples of universal triumph: Psalm 82:8, "Arise, O God, judge the earth: for thou shalt inherit all nations." Psalm 86:9, "All nations whom thou hast made shall come and worship before thee, O Lord; and shall glorify thy name." In Psalms 96, 98, 100, 117, and 148 all nations are urged to sing praises to God for his righteous reign upon the earth.

One of the most frequently quoted Psalms in the New Testament is Psalm 110. The first verse reads: "The Lord said unto my Lord, Sit thou at my right hand, until I make thine enemies thy footstool." The apostle Peter quotes this verse on the day of Pentecost. He declares that what happened at Pentecost was the fulfillment of Psalm 110:1. He did not interpret this as a cataclysmic act to be fulfilled at the day of judgment. He sees its fulfillment in the outpouring of the Holy Spirit upon the Church.

Thus the Psalms give a glorious picture of the future under the reign of the Messiah. There is no room for pessimism or defeatism. They give a wonderful commentary on the covenant promise to Abraham that all nations will be blessed. They look for the fulfillment in time and upon earth. Their faith was that the whole earth would be filled with the praises of God.

ISAIAH'S MILLENNIALISM

Even as the Psalms give us a picture of all nations blessed so does the Book of Isaiah. What a glorious prophecy is Isaiah 2:2-4: "And it shall come to pass in the last days, that the mountain of the Lord's house shall be established in the top of the mountains, and shall be exalted above the hills; and all nations shall flow unto it. And many people shall go and say, Come ye, and let us go up to the mountain of the Lord, to the house of the God of Jacob; and he will teach us of his ways, and we will walk in his paths: for out of Zion shall go forth the law, and the word of the Lord from Jerusalem. And he shall judge among the nations, and shall rebuke many people: and they shall beat their swords into plowshares, and their spears into pruninghooks: nation shall not lift sword against nation, neither shall they learn war any more." By no stretch of the imagination nor by an act of gymnastics can this prophecy be related to life in heaven. There are no weapons in heaven to be turned into plowshares. And surely there will be no occasion for nations to say: "Come and let us go up to heaven to learn the ways of God." This is a prophecy of what will happen upon earth in the Gospel dispensation.

That the millennial blessings are to be brought in by the Messiah is indicated in Isaiah 9:6, 7, "For unto us a child is born, unto us a son is given: and the government shall be upon his shoulder: and his name shall be called Wonderful, Counsellor, The mighty God, The everlasting Father, The Prince of Peace. Of the increase of his government and peace there shall be no end."

A millennial picture is also given to us in Isaiah 11. Through the reign of the "Branch" the wolf shall dwell with the lamb.

And in verse 9 it is stated: "They shall not hurt nor destroy in all my holy mountain: for the earth shall be full of the knowledge of the Lord, as the waters cover the sea." This is again a prophecy of the earth. It would be silly to prophesy that heaven, the dwelling place of God, will be filled with the knowledge of him as the waters cover the sea. It relates to the earth under the reign of the Messiah. In every place upon earth and in every nation God will be known.

It is upon Christ's atoning sacrifice that the victory of the Church is built. It is after Chapter 53 which gives such a clear picture of the vicarious atonement that we read these exultant words in Chapter 54: "Sing, O barren, thou that didst not bear; break forth into singing, and cry aloud, thou that didst not travail with child: for more are the children of the desolate than the children of the married wife, saith the Lord. Enlarge the place of thy tent, and let them stretch forth the curtains of thine habitations: spare not, lengthen thy cords, and strengthen thy stakes; For thou shalt break forth on the right hand and on the left; and thy seed shall inherit the Gentiles, and make the desolate cities to be inhabited. . . . No weapon that is formed against thee shall prosper."

From Isaiah 54 to 66 we have various pictures of the millennium. In these chapters we are informed of the destruction of Israel after the flesh for their refusal to behold and accept the Messiah. But this will not hinder the progress of the Gospel Church. For instance, it is stated to the Church in Isaiah 60:1, 3: "Arise, shine; for thy light is come, and the glory of the Lord is risen upon thee. . . . And the Gentiles shall come to thy light, and kings to the brightness of thy rising." And in Isaiah 62 is the vow of the Lord to accomplish it, "For Zion's sake will I not hold my peace, and for Jerusalem's sake I will not rest, until the righteousness thereof go forth as brightness, and the salvation thereof as a lamp that burneth, and the Gentiles shall see thy righteousness, and all kings thy glory." And we are urged to remind God of his vow in 62:6, 7, "Ye that make mention of the Lord, keep not silence, and give him no rest, till he establish, and till he make Jerusalem a praise in the earth."

We can challenge the Lord to fulfill the prophecies of Isaiah. We are to give God no rest till he makes the Church a praise throughout the earth. Of course, a Church which is ignorant of these promises, which evades the truth of them or dares not believe them, will never challenge God to bring about a universal peace through the spread of the Gospel.

THE NEW TESTAMENT

We have already shown how the Old Testament themes of triumph are carried on through the New Testament. The knowledge of Old Testament prophecy is taken for granted in the New Testament. We have already mentioned that Luke 10 indicates the fall of Satan through the preaching of the Gospel and that Romans 16:20 reveals that Satan will be crushed under the feet of the Church. Revelation 12:9, 11 states the defeat of Satan through the preaching of the blood of Christ. There are passages like Col. 2:15; Heb. 2:14; 1 John 3:8 that bring out the triumph of Christ. There is Romans 4:13 to the effect that the Church is the heir of the world and Christ states that the meek will inherit the earth. His great commission implies the fulfillment of the covenant promise through the preaching and teaching of the gospel. Paul is able to say in 2 Cor. 2:14, "Now thanks be unto God, which always causeth us to triumph in Christ, and maketh manifest the savour of his knowledge by us in every place."

There are the parables such as the mustard seed and the leaven. The grain of mustard seed, which though the least of all seeds, is the greatest of herbs. The leaven pervaded the whole. Both of these parables indicate the slow but progressive growth of the kingdom of God. Both point to the ultimate triumph of the Gospel.

Romans 11 surely speaks of the conversion of Israel after the flesh. If the fall of the Jews brought richness to the Gentiles how much will it add to the riches of the Gentiles when the Jews are restored. It will be like life from the dead. I have never been able to understand how people can interpret the "fulness of the Gentiles" to be the emptiness or poverty of the Gentiles. When the Gentile world is converted then will come about the conversion of the Jews as a nation.

The Book of Revelation, of course, is the book which speaks of the ultimate triumph of Christ and his Church. Terrible ignorance of this book causes some to think it speaks only of a triumph by a cataclysmic act at the second coming of our Lord. The poor Church, according to some, is only to struggle without hope till that Day. Rightly interpreted Revelation reveals a triumph of the Church in time and history. It sums up for us the promise of Genesis 3:15; it gives reason to the triumphant poetry of the Psalter; it indicates the fulfillment of the covenant promise that all nations will be blessed.

TILL WE ALL

"Till we all come in the unity of the faith, and of the knowledge of the Son of God, unto a perfect man, unto the measure of the stature of the fulness of Christ" is the evangelical ecumenical goal. The apostle Paul set that goal before the infant church at Ephesus. One catches the sound of the certainty of arrival by the firm expression, *Till we all come*. Paul was not speaking about the hereafter for in the previous verses of Ephesians 4 he informed that church that Christ "gave some, apostles; and some, prophets; and some, evangelists; and some, pastors and teachers; for the perfecting of the saints, for the work of the ministry, for the edifying of the body of Christ." And the purpose was "That we henceforth be no more children, tossed to and fro, and carried about with every wind of doctrine, by the sleight of men, and cunning craftiness whereby they lie in wait to deceive." This, alas, refers to a condition upon the evil earth. Yet the definite certainty of accomplishment is in the "till we all come." The attainment of "the measure of the stature of the fulness of Christ" is ever before the church.

"Till we all come," indicates that we are travelling towards the promised land: *the stature of the fulness of Christ*. The Church is still in the wilderness, maturing under severe trials and temptations. Israel could have entered into the land of promise immediately but lost faith at the thought of fearful giants who possessed the promised land. Lacking faith they refused to go forward to possess the land and were condemned to travel through the wilderness. Evangelicals are prone to think that the heathen possess such power that they cannot be vanquished. But the earth is the Lord's and the fulness thereof.

Christ is more powerful than Satan; truth is more powerful than falsehood; and light is more powerful than darkness.

Dr. J. H. Thornwell wrote this thrilling passage, "If the Church could be aroused to a deeper sense of the glory that awaits her, she would enter with a warmer spirit into the struggles that are before her. Hope would inspire ardour. She would even now arise from the dust, and like the eagle plume her pinions for loftier flights than she has yet taken. What she wants, and what every individual Christian wants, is faith—faith in her sublime vocation, in her Divine resources, in the presence and efficacy of the Spirit that dwells in her—faith in the truth, faith in Jesus, and faith in God. With such a faith there would be no need to speculate about the future. That would speedily reveal itself. It is our unfaithfulness, our negligence and unbelief, our low and carnal aims, that retard the chariot of the Redeemer. The Bridegroom cannot come until the Bride has made herself ready. Let the Church be in earnest after greater holiness in her own members, and in faith and love undertake the conquest of the world, and she will soon settle the question whether her resources are competent to change the face of the earth" (*Collected Writings* (1871), Vol. II, p. 48).

It should not be doubted that times of refreshing will come as the Church of Jesus Christ exercises faith and prays earnestly that an outpouring of the Holy Spirit may invigorate her afresh and cause the church to spring out of its withered and weak state to evangelize the world. The Church should engage in prayer that the ministry may be faithful in preaching the whole counsel of God "Till we all come in the unity of the faith, and of the knowledge of the Son of God, unto a perfect man, unto the measure of the stature of the fulness of Christ."

Date Due